Strategies to Integrate the *Arts* in Language Arts

Authors

Jennifer M. Bogard, M.Ed.
Lisa Donovan, Ph.D.

LESLEY UNIVERSITY

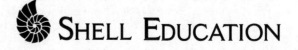

SHELL EDUCATION

Publishing Credits

Dona Herweck Rice, *Editor-in-Chief*; Robin Erickson, *Production Director*;
Lee Aucoin, *Creative Director*; Timothy J. Bradley, *Illustration Manager*;
Sara Johnson, M.S.Ed., *Editorial Director*; Tracy Edmunds, *Editor*;
Leah Quillian, *Assistant Editor*; Grace Alba, *Designer*;
Corinne Burton, *M.A.Ed., Publisher*

Contributing Authors

David Williams, M.Ed., Grade 4 Teacher, Newbury Elementary School, MA
Brittany Williams, M.Ed., Grade 3 Teacher, Newbury Elementary School, MA
Amy Ludwig VanDerwater, Writer and Writing Teacher, http://www.amylv.com
Tanya West, Music Teacher, Theater Manager and Director, MSAD 35

Consultants

Mary Ann Cappiello, Ed.D., Associate Professor of Language and Literacy, Lesley University
Louise Pascale, Ph.D., Associate Professor, Creative Arts in Learning, Lesley University
Rebecca E. Woodman, M.Ed., Speech and Language Pathologist, Central Elementary School, South Berwick, ME
Principal Vicki Stewart, M.Ed., MSAD 35
Principal Nina D'Aran, B.S., Elementary Education, MA Counseling Psychology, Doctoral Candidate Educational
    Leadership, Central School, South Berwick, Maine
Celeste Miller, M.F.A., Choreographer, adjunct faculty, Creative Arts in Learning Division, Lesley University
Grace S. Jacobs, M.Ed., MSAD 35
Jim McGuinness, Ed.D., Literacy Specialist, Falmouth, MA PSD and Adjunct Faculty, Lesley University
Janeth W. Franklin, M.A., Doctoral Candidate, Walden University, Adjunct Faculty, Glendale Community College,
    Glendale, AZ, Staff Developer in Mind, Brain and Education Science

Image Credits
All images Shutterstock

Standards
© 2004 Mid-continent Research for Education and Learning (McREL)
© 2007 Teachers of English to Speakers of Other Languages, Inc. (TESOL)
© 2007 Board of Regents of the University of Wisconsin System. World-Class Instructional Design and Assessment
    (WIDA). For more information on using the WIDA ELP Standards, please visit the WIDA website at www.wida.us.
© 2010 National Governors Association Center for Best Practices and Council of Chief State School Officers (CCSS)

Shell Education
5301 Oceanus Drive
Huntington Beach, CA 92649-1030
http://www.shelleducation.com
ISBN 978-1-4258-1090-0
© 2013 Shell Educational Publishing, Inc.

Table of Contents

The Importance of Arts Integration

Teachers have an important and challenging job, and it seems they are asked to do more with each passing year. Lesley professors in the Creative Arts Division hear from teachers regularly that integrating the arts would be a great thing to do if they just had the time and support. Yet research shows that the integration of the arts is an efficient and effective strategy for addressing some of the greatest challenges in today's educational landscape as the arts deepen learning in ways that engage all learners of all abilities and needs (President's Committee on the Arts and the Humanities 2011; Burnaford 2007). Study after study points to compelling evidence of the significant outcomes that are linked to arts integration.

According to the President's Committee on the Arts and the Humanities, "studies have now documented significant links between arts integration models and academic and social outcomes for students, efficacy for teachers, and school-wide improvements in culture and climate. Arts integration is efficient, addressing a number of outcomes at the same time. Most important, the greatest gains in schools with arts integration are often seen school-wide and also with the most hard-to-reach and economically disadvantaged students" (2011).

A recent study funded by the Ford Foundation and led by researchers from Lesley University's Creative Arts in Learning Division and an external advisory team conducted research with over 200 Lesley alumni teaching across the country who had been trained in arts-integration strategies. The findings suggest that arts-integrated teaching provides a variety of strategies for accessing content and expressing understanding of learning that is culturally responsive and relevant in students' lives. This leads to deep learning, increased student ownership, and engagement with academic content. Not only does arts integration engage students in creativity, innovation, and imagination, it renews teachers' commitment to teaching (Bellisario and Donovan with Prendergast 2012).

Really then, the question becomes this: *How can we afford not to provide students with access to the arts as an engaging way to learn and to express ideas across the curriculum?*

Arts integration is the investigation of curricular content through artistic explorations where the arts provide an avenue for rigorous investigation, representation, expression, and reflection of both curricular content and the art form itself (Diaz, Donovan, and Pascale 2006). This book provides teachers with concrete strategies to integrate the arts across the curriculum. Arts-integration strategies are introduced with contextual information about the art form (creative movement, drama, music, poetry, storytelling, and visual arts).

The Importance of Arts Integration *(cont.)*

Each art form provides you with innovative strategies to help students fully engage with and connect to the content area under consideration. Creative movement allows students to embody ideas and work conceptually. Drama challenges students to explore multiple perspectives of characters, historical figures, and scientists. Music develops students' ability to listen, to generate a sense of community, and to communicate and connect aurally. Poetry invites students to build a more playful, fresh relationship with written and spoken language. Storytelling connects us with our roots in the oral tradition and heightens our awareness of the role of story in our lives. Visual art taps into our ability to observe critically, envision, think through metaphor, and build visual literacy in a world where images are pervasive.

Providing learners with the opportunity to investigate curriculum and express their understanding with the powerful languages of the arts will deepen students' understanding, heighten their curiosity, and bring forward their voices as they interact more fully with content and translate their ideas into new forms. This book is a beginning, a "way in."

We invite you to see for yourself by bringing the strategies shared in this book to your classroom and seeing what happens. We hope this resource leaves you looking for deeper experiences with the arts both for you and for your students.

What Does It Mean to Integrate the Arts?

We believe that a vital path to encouraging students to become literate in the twenty-first century is through the integration of the English language arts and the arts and that active involvement in the arts can help learners develop and use creative and purposeful expression in language, explore different perspectives, and internalize new ideas and ways of thinking. Yellin, Jones, and DeVries assert that critical comprehension happens when the reader is "able to integrate his or her own thinking with the information from the text," allowing him or her to visualize events in the text and to "respond creatively through art, music, drama, and writing" (2007).

Listening, speaking, reading, writing, viewing, and visual representation are important components of the English language arts (Yellin, Jones, and DeVries 2007). The Common Core State Standards for English Language Arts (National Governors Association Center for Best Practices and Council of Chief State School Officers 2011) guide students to "develop the skills in reading, writing, speaking, and listening that are the foundation for any creative and purposeful expression in language." Skills in reading, writing, speaking, listening, language, and media and technology determine what it means to be literate in the twenty-first century. Albers and Harste make the point that "in light of this changing world of texts and the diverse student population, there is a need to redefine literacy" (2007, 8).

The Importance of Arts Integration (cont.)

Mary Clare Powell, poet and former director of the Lesley University Creative Arts Division, agrees, noting that "the arts help teachers become multilingual, because the arts are many languages. You can say things in music that you cannot translate into words: When you dance a concept, it is not the same as when you speak about it. The visual arts are their own particular language, not a shortcut for words" (1997).

This book harnesses the power of the arts to provide you with engaging strategies for students to access curriculum, to explore content, and to represent their learning. We will guide you in the use of the arts and provide a context in which language arts ideas take shape and deepen while the arts inform and enrich the lives of your students. We do not want you to do this in a tangential manner or just on an enrichment basis. Rather, we want you to use arts integration as an approach to teaching the most prevalent standards in your English language arts curriculum and to do so frequently. In teaching ideas through artistic explorations, you will help your students develop skills and knowledge in both disciplines. We will share strategies with you that are flexible enough to be used across content strands and grade levels.

Why Should I Integrate the Arts?

Reading, along with mathematics, continues to dominate classroom instruction and mandated assessments. Government-led initiatives such as the Common Core State Standards and No Child Left Behind underscore the importance of English language arts skills throughout all subject areas. Teachers of all subjects share the responsibility and have a role in this interdisciplinary approach to teaching literacy. For example, the Common Core literacy standards for grades K–5 apply to a range of subjects and in grades 6 and above call upon teachers of content areas, such as history/social studies, science, and technical subjects, to teach students skills in reading, writing, speaking, listening, and language. Students are expected to read, write, speak, listen, and use language effectively throughout the curriculum.

With our curriculum dominated by reading and mathematics, little room is left for the arts. Yet as educators, we want to teach the whole child. Students need both the arts and academic disciplines. Research suggests that academic achievement may be linked to the arts (Kennedy 2006). As noted by Douglas Reeves, "the challenge for school leaders is to offer every student a rich experience with the arts without sacrificing the academic opportunities students need" (2007, 80). By integrating the arts with English language arts, we are able to place language arts ideas within rich settings and provide students with access to the arts. In fact, the arts can lead to "deep learning" in which students are more genuinely engaged with academic content, spend more time on task, and take ownership of their learning (Bellisario and Donovan with Prendergast 2012).

The Importance of Arts Integration (cont.)

Rinne et al. (2011) identify several ways in which arts integration improves long-term retention through elaboration, enactment, and rehearsal. Specifically, when learners create and add details to their own visual models, dramatize a concept or skill, sing a song repeatedly, or rehearse for a performance, they are increasing the likelihood that they will remember what they have learned. This retention lasts not just for the next chapter test but also over significant periods of time. Think about how children learn the order of the alphabet or how you might remember the number of days in a month. Through repetition that does not feel like "drill and kill," this information is retained for life because students become deeply engaged when working in arts integration. They eagerly revisit, review, rehearse, edit, and work through ideas repeatedly and in authentic ways as they translate ideas into new forms.

As brain research deepens our understanding of how learning takes place, educators have come to better appreciate the importance of the arts. The arts support communication, emotional connections, community, and higher-order thinking. They are also linked to increased academic achievement, especially among at-risk students. Eric Jensen (2001) argues that "the arts enhance the process of learning. The systems they nourish, which include our integrated sensory, attentional, cognitive, emotional, and motor capabilities, are, in fact, the driving forces behind all other learning." Lessons and activities that integrate English language arts and the arts provide a rich environment for the exploration of English language arts ideas for all students and particularly for those students who need new ways to access curriculum and to express understanding as well as providing another source of motivation.

Teaching through the arts provides authentic differentiated learning for every student in the classroom. As neurologist Todd Rose notes (2012), all learners learn in variable ways. The Center for Applied Special Technology (http://www.cast.org/about/index.html) suggests that in meeting the needs of variable learners, educators should expand their teaching to provide universal design. That is, teachers should include strategies that "are flexible and responsive to the needs of all learners" by providing "multiple means of engagement, methods of presentation of content and multiple avenues for expression of understanding." The integration of the arts provides opportunities to address all three universal design principles.

For example, the process of enacting a scene from a text provides a meaningful opportunity for metacognition, or "what a child knows about his or her own thinking and how the child is able to monitor that thinking" (Yellin, Jones, and DeVries 2007). Imagine students who, as they prepare to enact a scene from a book, determine what parts of the reading are unclear, go back through the text and reread, visualize the events, and visualize themselves performing the scene. Arts integration not only benefits students by deepening their connection to content and fostering interdisciplinary learning in the arts and English language arts but also promotes what the Partnership for 21st Century Skills (2011) researchers note as the 4 Cs: creativity, critical thinking, communication, and collaboration. Arts integration brings these significant benefits to learning and also engages teachers and students in curiosity, imagination, and passion for learning.

Arts and the Standards

Connections to the Common Core State Standards for English Language Arts

Within the Common Core State Standards for English Language Arts are seven descriptions that characterize the "literate individual." Through the Common Core Standards in reading, writing, speaking, listening, and language, students exhibit the following capacities (National Governors Association Center for Best Practices and Council of Chief State School Officers 2011):

1. They demonstrate independence.
2. They build strong content knowledge.
3. They respond to the varying demands of audience, task, purpose, and discipline.
4. They comprehend as well as critique.
5. They value evidence.
6. They use technology and digital media strategically and capably.
7. They come to understand other perspectives and cultures.

These practices are intended to be interwoven with the content standards and can be thought of as the habits of mind we want to develop in our students. As students represent English language arts ideas in artistic forms, they are involved in applying and demonstrating these seven capacities.

Artistic Habits of Mind

As well as language arts habits of mind, students will also be developing these artistic habits of mind (Hetland et al. 2007). With these habits of mind, students are able to:

1. Develop craft
2. Engage and persist
3. Envision
4. Express
5. Observe
6. Reflect
7. Stretch and explore
8. Understand the art world

Though these habits were identified in an investigation of visual art practices, they are relevant for the practice of all of the arts.

It is important to note that the skills that are significant parts of what the arts develop are valued in every field. The arts develop these skills naturally as students explore and translate ideas into artistic forms. Researcher Lois Hetland notes that "it is these qualities—intrinsic to the arts—that are valued in every domain but not necessarily taught in those subjects in school. That's what makes the arts such potent resources for teaching valued dispositions—what the arts teach well is not used uniquely in the arts but is valuable across a wide spectrum of contexts" (2009, 37).

Arts and the Standards *(cont.)*

Classroom Environment

A safe classroom environment is needed for language arts ideas and artistic expressions to flourish. Learners must feel comfortable to make mistakes, to critique the work of others, and to celebrate success. Think back to groups to which you have presented new ideas or creative works. How did you feel as you waited for their reactions? What was it about their behavior that made you feel more or less comfortable? What was it about your thinking that made you feel more or less safe? Such reflections will lead you to ways you can talk about these ideas with your students. As teachers, we must be role models for our students as we model our willingness to take risks and engage in new ways of learning. You will find that the arts by their nature invite risk taking, experimentation, and self-discipline as well as encourage the development of a supportive learning community.

Developing a learning community in which learners support and respect one another takes time, but there are things that you can do to help support its development:

- **Establish clear expectations for respect.** Respect is nonnegotiable. As students engage in creative explorations, it is crucial that they honor one another's ideas, invite all voices to the table, and discuss the work in ways that value each contribution. Self-discipline and appreciation for fellow students' creative work is often a beneficial outcome of arts integration (Bellisario and Donovan with Prendergast 2012). Take time for students to brainstorm ways in which they can show one another respect and what they can do when they feel that they have not been respected. Work with students to create guidelines for supporting the creative ideas of others and agree to uphold them as a group.

- **Explore several ice breakers** during the first weeks of school that allow students to get to know one another informally and begin to discover interests they have in common. As students learn more about one another, they develop a sense of themselves as individuals and as a classroom unit and are more apt to want to support one another. Using fun, dynamic warm-ups not only helps students get their brains working but also builds a sense of community and support for risk taking.

- **Tell your students about ways in which you are engaged in learning new ideas.** Talk about your realizations and challenges along the way, and demonstrate your own willingness to take risks and persevere.

- **Find ways to support the idea that we can all act, draw, sing, rhyme, and so forth.** Avoid saying negative things about your own art or language arts skill levels, and emphasize your continuous growth.

Arts and the Standards *(cont.)*

- **Learn to ask open-ended questions rather than give answers**. By asking a question like, "What does this symbol represent to you?," students are able to articulate, refocus, or clarify their own thinking.

- **Avoid judgments**. Students who are trying to earn your praise for their artistic products will not take the risks necessary for creative work. Encourage students to reflect on their own goals and whether they think they have met them.

- **Emphasize process over product**. Enormous learning and discovery takes place during the creative process. This is as significant as the final product that is produced and in some cases even more so.

How This Book Is Organized

Strategies

The strategies and model lessons in this book are organized within six art modalities:

- creative movement

- drama

- music

- poetry

- storytelling

- visual arts

Within each modality, five strategies are presented that integrate that art form with the teaching of language arts. The strategies are not intended as an exhaustive list but rather as exemplary ways to integrate the arts into language arts.

Though we have provided a model lesson for each strategy, these strategies are flexible and can be used in a variety of ways across a variety of content areas. These models will allow you to try out the ideas with your students and to envision many other ways to adapt these strategies for use in your teaching. For example, we explored painter Georgia O'Keeffe's decision to move to New York City in our drama strategy of monologues, but you may prefer to integrate the monologue strategy with other areas of language arts such as the exploration of a historical character's decision during a significant world history event. The strategy of juxtaposition could be associated with any of the arts as we can juxtapose movements, characters, sounds, words, perspectives, or materials. As you become familiar and comfortable using the strategies, you may combine a variety of them across the art modalities within a lesson. For example, you might have students begin with writing a monologue but then draw out words and phrases to create a poem that distills the main ideas the character is exploring or create a movement phrase that depicts twists and turns in the monologue. The goal is to make the choices that best fit you and your students.

How This Book Is Organized (*cont.*)

Organization of the Lessons

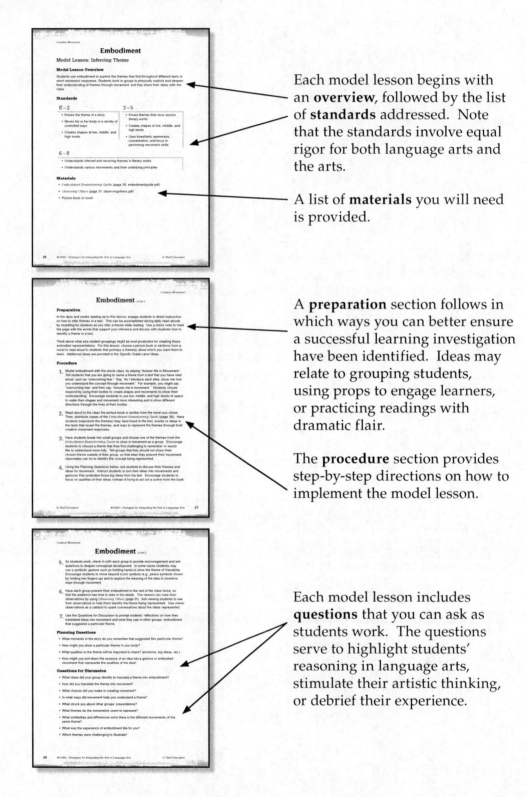

Each model lesson begins with an **overview**, followed by the list of **standards** addressed. Note that the standards involve equal rigor for both language arts and the arts.

A list of **materials** you will need is provided.

A **preparation** section follows in which ways you can better ensure a successful learning investigation have been identified. Ideas may relate to grouping students, using props to engage learners, or practicing readings with dramatic flair.

The **procedure** section provides step-by-step directions on how to implement the model lesson.

Each model lesson includes **questions** that you can ask as students work. The questions serve to highlight students' reasoning in language arts, stimulate their artistic thinking, or debrief their experience.

How This Book Is Organized *(cont.)*

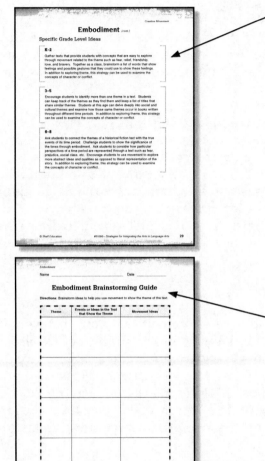

Specific grade level ideas follow with suggestions on how to better meet the needs of students within the K–2, 3–5, 6–8, and 9–12 grade levels. They may also suggest other ways to explore or extend the ideas in the model lesson at these levels. Read all of the sections as an idea written for a different grade span may suggest something you want to do with your students.

At least one **reproducible** is provided for each model lesson. Often in the form of graphic organizers, the reproducibles are designed to help students brainstorm ideas, organize and record their thinking, or reflect on their learning. Reproducibles are available on the Digital Resource CD in PDF form and oftentimes as Word documents to allow for customization of content and text for students of diverse abilities and needs.

How This Book Is Organized (cont.)

How to Use the Lessons

These strategies can be used to teach language arts in any K–12 classroom with any language arts curriculum. A strategy lesson can be implemented as a way to deepen or expand the exploration of a topic, or if you have the flexibility, expanded to several days or a week. You may choose to use the strategy lesson within your language arts lesson, in combination with time assigned to the arts, or when considering storytelling or poetry, perhaps in conjunction with other content areas.

You may wish to focus on one art form at a time to help yourself become familiar with using that art modality to teach language arts. Or you may want to look through the content index and explore models that relate to what you are teaching now or are about to teach. Over time, you will become familiar with the strategies and find that you choose to integrate them on a regular basis. If integrating arts and language arts is new to you, consider working with another teacher to explore the ideas together. Collaborate with teachers of art, dance, drama, or music in your school system to draw from their expertise in deepening the artistic work.

Working with Text Sets

We know the power of mentor texts and have recommended books that work well with particular strategies (see Appendix C: Recommended Resources), but we also encourage you to draw from a variety of texts such as newspapers, web-based resources, cooking recipes, and primary and secondary sources. Think of artwork as text as it provides worlds to be explored (e.g., painting, musical scores, plays, choreographed work, and poems). This allows students to engage with a variety of complex texts. Engaging in the arts promotes the kind of "close reading" that complex text requires (Varlas 2012).

Text complexity and growth in comprehension are key features of the Common Core State Standards. According to the Common Core State Standards, "the Reading standards place equal emphasis on the sophistication of what students read and the skill with which they read. Standard 10 defines a grade-by-grade 'staircase' of increasing text complexity that rises from beginning reading to the college and career readiness level. Whatever they are reading, students must also show a steadily growing ability to discern more from and make fuller use of text, including making an increasing number of connections among ideas and between texts, considering a wider range of textual evidence, and becoming more sensitive to inconsistencies, ambiguities, and poor reasoning in texts" (National Governors Association Center for Best Practices and Council of Chief State School Officers 2011).

For each lesson, we encourage working with text sets and resources from multiple genres and modalities. Cappiello and Dawes discuss "multimodal, multigenre" text sets (2013), explaining that a text set draws from various modalities, including print, audio, photographs, artifacts, webcams, and podcasts. By *multigenre*, they suggest diverse forms of writing, such as a blog, in addition to traditional genres, such as books and magazines. Text sets may include nonfiction, fiction, poetry, and more to present a wide view of one topic and the approaches of multiple authors.

How This Book Is Organized (cont.)

Assessment

Data-driven decision making, documentation of learning, and meeting benchmarks are all phrases referring to assessment practices that are embedded in our schools. Assessment has become a time-consuming activity for all involved in education, and yet the time and effort spent does not always yield what is needed to improve learning. As you think about how to assess lessons and activities that integrate language arts and the arts, it is important to stop and consider how to best use assessment to increase learning for your students. It is most likely that in addressing that goal, you will also be documenting learning in ways that can be shared with students, parents, administrators, and other interested stakeholders.

We encourage you to focus on formative assessment, that is, assessment that is incorporated throughout the process of learning. This assessment will inform your instructional decisions during the process of teaching. The purpose of this assessment is to provide feedback for learners and teachers along the way in addition to assessment of learning at the end. As such, we are most interested in the data collected during the learning process as well as after it is completed. The goals are to make the learning process visible, to determine the depth of understanding, and to note the process the students undergo as they translate their knowledge of language arts into an art form or explore language arts ideas through the arts.

There are a variety of tools you can use to gather data to support your instructional decision making:

- **Ask questions to draw out, clarify, and probe students' thinking**. The questions in each strategy section will provide you with ideas on which you can elaborate. Use questioning to make on-the-spot adjustments to your plans as well as to identify learning moments as they are unfolding. This can be as simple as posing a new question or as complex as bringing a few students together for a mini-lesson.

- **Walk around with a clipboard or notebook** so that you can easily capture students' comments and questions as well as your own observations. Too often, we think we will remember students' words only to find ourselves unable to reproduce them at a later time. These annotations will allow you to note patterns within a student's remarks or among students' comments. They can suggest misconceptions that provide you with an entry to the next day's work through a comment such as, "Yesterday, some of you wondered whether a reader has to read nonfiction text in sequential order. Let's explore that today." A suggested template is provided in Appendix B (page 238) and available on the Digital Resource CD (notetaking.pdf). Make several copies and attach them to a clipboard.

- **Use the graphic organizers in the model lessons** as support for the creative process. Using these forms, have students brainstorm ideas for their art product and their language arts connections. These organizers provide a snapshot of students' thinking at a point in the creative process.

How This Book Is Organized (cont.)

- **Use a camera to document student learning**. Each of the strategies leads to a creative product but not necessarily one that provides a tangible artifact or one that fits on a standard size piece of paper. Use a digital camera to take numerous pictures that can capture, for example, a piece of visual art at various stages of development or the gestures actors and storytellers use in their dramatic presentations. Similarly, use video to capture planning sessions, group discussions, and final presentations. As well as documenting learning, collecting such evidence helps students reflect back on their learning. Consider developing a learning portfolio for your students that they can review and add to over time.

- Recognize that although each strategy leads to a final creative product, it, too, can be used to inform future instruction. **Comparisons can be made across products to note student growth**.

- **Make students an integral part of the assessment process**. Provide them with opportunities to reflect on their work. For quick, formative reflections, ask students to respond simply; for example, say, "Hold up 1–4 fingers to show me how well you think you represented language arts ideas in your picture." Have students reflect in more complex ways as well. For example, have students choose artifacts to include in their portfolio and explain the reasons for their choices. Have students reflect on their work as a class. For example, ask, "How well did we build on one another's language arts ideas today? How well did we support one another's creative thinking?" Encourage discussion of artistic work to not only draw out what students have learned in their own creative process but also how and what they learned from the work of their peers. In this way, students teach and learn from one another.

- **Design rubrics that help you organize your assessment data.** A well-crafted rubric can help you gather data more quickly as well as increase the likelihood that you are being equitable in your evaluation of assessment data. Select criteria to assess learning in language arts as well as in the art form because arts integration supports equal rigor both in content and in the arts.

Arts integration deepens learning both in the content area being explored and in the art form being used. In a third-grade classroom at the Sumner School in Roslindale, Massachusetts, students were exploring character traits during a lesson about Amelia Earhart. First, students read a series of texts based on the life of this groundbreaking female pilot. Next, students were asked to consider text-to-self connections by creating a frozen sculpture with their bodies (the tableaux strategy), showing a character trait that they felt represented some aspect of them. This generated a sense of the relevance of character traits and teased out a wide range of personalities and qualities. Students thought hard about what might represent their individual character traits and were thoroughly engrossed in sharing their own traits as well as considering the traits of their peers. Next, students formed small groups and brainstormed character traits of Amelia Earhart. They analyzed the texts for evidence of these traits, eagerly revisiting the text as they planned what scene they would create to demonstrate the trait in action. When set to the task, the room was abuzz with conversation about what scene would best bring to life the selected traits. As students made choices about how to bring their

How This Book Is Organized (cont.)

ideas to life through images, the conversation moved between ideas about intangible concepts such as bravery and how these ideas could be translated into specific images. Each group created a tableau scene depicting a moment when the character trait was exemplified. The still images created included vivid scenes from the text.

Soundscapes is another strategy to engage learners. Students in a third-grade classroom explored the concept of setting in *The Tin Forest* by Helen Ward. The teacher told students that she would be reading the text aloud without showing the pictures just yet, and she asked them to create mental images and to imagine the sounds, smells, tastes, sensations, and memories that were triggered as they listened. Next, the teacher asked students to share some of their mental images and to recall specific words from the text that allowed them to imagine the scene, such as strong verbs, snapshots (Lane 1992), thoughtshots (Lane 1992), similes, and metaphors.

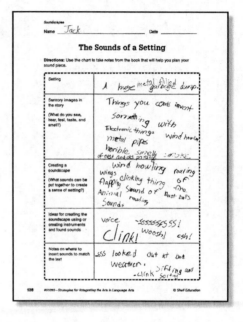

Next, the teacher shared the rich and evocative illustrations by Chris Anderson, and students mined the images for details that deepened their comprehension. For the opening scene of the book, students shared a wide range of responses:

> *Sounds:* beats of sad music; the sound of metal scraping; the sound of digging—a shovel against soil; the sounds of the old man's deep sighs

> *Tastes:* taste of rust and smoke-filled air

> *Smells:* heavy, slow moving, smoke-filled air

> *Sensations:* the feeling of cold, damp weather on skin; pinpricks of rain; wet soil; damp paper

> *Images:* gray landscape filled with metal pieces of all sizes, wires, electronic devices; potato peelings, half-eaten food; a ramshackle shed; a hunched-over, wrinkled man of 101 years; images of corrugated tin rooftops

Following this exploration, students were asked to identify found objects with which to create a soundscape that would establish a sense of place in the story.

Students collected a wide range of materials: aluminum foil to be scrunched, a metal grater with a spoon for banging and scraping, rustling paper to make soft rain sounds, shoes to make footsteps, and a bucket of soil and a small spade to create the sound of digging. Also included in the soundscape was the sound of soft claps and vocal sounds that simulated the crackle of a fire. Three groups created soundscapes to illuminate

How This Book Is Organized (cont.)

different moments in the story. Then, as the teacher read the text again, the students performed their soundscapes as their setting was introduced while the rest of the class experienced the story and soundscape with eyes closed.

"I felt like I was there!" one student exclaimed at the end of the story. "The sounds totally made me feel the place," said another.

As there are so many aspects of this task to capture, a rubric can be quite helpful. A suggested rubric is provided in Appendix B (page 239) and on the Digital Resource CD (assessmentrubric.pdf). Observation protocols help teachers document evidence of student learning, something all teachers must do. A variety of forms could be used, and it is not possible to include all areas that you might attend to in an interdisciplinary lesson. Two suggested forms are included in Appendix B and provided on the Digital Resource CD, built on the work of Collins (2012a, 2012b) and Dacey (2012a, 2012b, 2012c, 2012d). One form is for use with individual students (page 240, individualform.pdf) and one for use with groups (page 241, groupform.pdf).

Correlation to the Standards

Shell Education is committed to producing educational materials that are research and standards based. In this effort, we have correlated all of our products to the academic standards of all 50 United States, the District of Columbia, the Department of Defense Dependent Schools, and all Canadian provinces.

How to Find Standards Correlations

To print a customized correlation report of this product for your state, visit our website at http://www.shelleducation.com and follow the on-screen directions. If you require assistance in printing correlation reports, please contact Customer Service at 1-877-777-3450.

Purpose and Intent of Standards

Legislation mandates that all states adopt academic standards that identify the skills students will learn in kindergarten through grade twelve. Many states also have standards for Pre-K. This same legislation sets requirements to ensure the standards are detailed and comprehensive.

Standards are designed to focus instruction and guide adoption of curricula. Standards are statements that describe the criteria necessary for students to meet specific academic goals. They define the knowledge, skills, and content students should acquire at each level. Standards are also used to develop standardized tests to evaluate students' academic progress. Teachers are required to demonstrate how their lessons meet state standards. State standards are used in the development of all of our products, so educators can be assured they meet the academic requirements of each state.

Common Core State Standards

The lessons in this book are aligned to the Common Core State Standards (CCSS). The standards support the objectives presented throughout the lessons and are provided on the Digital Resource CD (standards.pdf).

McREL Compendium

We use the Mid-continent Research for Education and Learning (McREL) Compendium to create standards correlations. Each year, McREL analyzes state standards and revises the compendium. By following this procedure, McREL is able to produce a general compilation of national standards. Each lesson in this product is based on one or more McREL standards, which are also provided on the Digital Resource CD (standards.pdf).

TESOL and WIDA Standards

The lessons in this book promote English language development for English language learners. The standards correlations can be found on the Digital Resource CD (standards.pdf).

Correlation to the Standards (cont.)

The main focus of the lessons presented in this book is to promote the integration of the arts in language arts. The standards for both the arts and language arts are provided on the Digital Resource CD (standards.pdf).

Common Core State Standards

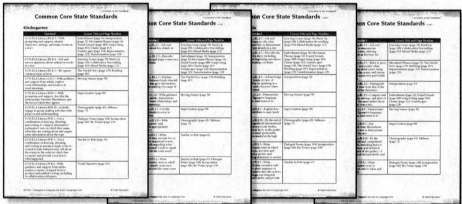

McREL Standards

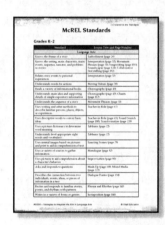
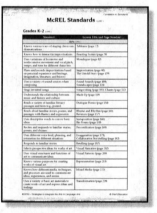

TESOL and WIDA Standards

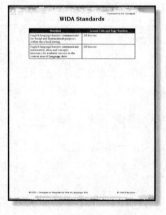

Creative Movement

Creative Movement

Understanding Creative Movement

Integrating creative movement across the curriculum is an engaging approach to learning that allows students to experience, translate, and communicate language arts ideas kinesthetically. In 1983, Howard Gardner identified bodily-kinesthetic intelligence within his theory of multiple intelligences (2011) as one way that students learn. Neuroscientists are finding that memory and recall are improved when the body is engaged in the learning process (Zull 2002) and that the mind uses the body to make sense of ideas (Carpenter 2010).

While important for all learners, opportunities to express themselves nonverbally can be particularly powerful for some students. Such opportunities can provide students with access to language arts content that would not be possible otherwise. Stacey Skoning (2008) states that creative movement, or dance, "is important to incorporate into our inclusive classrooms if we want to meet the needs of more diverse groups of students."

Creative movement allows students to be physically active, which often increases students' attention span, but it is much more than just the incorporation of movement into classroom activities. When students are involved in creative movement, they become more mindful of their bodies' ability to communicate, explore what happens when they move with intention, engage in problem solving through movement, and develop awareness of their creative choices. It is important to keep the possibilities for this work in mind as your students explore these lessons.

As students deconstruct and reconstruct concepts, they take ownership of the ideas through kinesthetic means and creative choices. Writer and choreographer Susan Griss (1994) makes the point that because creative movement is "expressive, informative, and analytical," it can heighten learning in the language arts classroom by increasing comprehension, by supporting the development of whole language skills, by providing multicultural insigts, by bolstering social skills, and by changing energy into creative outlets.

Creative Movement (cont.)

Strategies for Creative Movement

✍ Embodiment

In this strategy, students use shapes (body shapes, lines, angles, curves), level (low, middle, high), and movement or gesture to *embody*, or show with their bodies, their understanding of concepts and terms. The strategy can be used to model complex ideas, helping students to grasp, investigate, and internalize concepts. Students can also create spontaneous creative movement to help them summarize or review their learning.

Working with others to embody ideas in movement can prompt students to discuss characteristics of a particular concept, both as they translate ideas into movement and also while they view the presentation of other groups' ideas. Dance artist Celeste Miller (Miller, pers. comm. 2012) suggests that the language of movement can provide a "palette for expression of both abstract and tangible ideas." Having groups of students embody the same concept allows them to see how different movement interpretations can convey the same ideas. Coming up with more than one approach for depicting an idea encourages creative and critical thinking. This strategy can help students solidify ideas and help you assess students' depth of understanding.

✍ Interpretation

In this strategy, students explore and interpret emotion and internal thought processes through abstract movement that symbolizes internal processes. As characters are explored, students embody internal thinking processes, qualities of character traits, and character motivation. Students explore parallels in movement qualities with a variety of emotional states. Additionally, they explore the qualities of emotion, how things change over time, and how a character's choices can be driven by emotion and character traits.

✍ Moving Statues

This strategy combines held poses with movement as students incorporate the use of shape (body shapes, lines, angles, curves), level (low, medium, high), and quality of movement (characteristics such as sustained, swing, percussive, collapsed), allowing them to make nuanced changes in movements. Students can form moving statues alone, in pairs, or in groups.

A group statue results in a large fluid representation of a concept as students create an evolving model of the idea being explored. Moving statues can also require students to position themselves in relation to others. Through such experiences, creative movement can improve self-esteem and social functioning in addition to deepening understanding of language arts content (Theodorakou and Zervas 2003).

Creative Movement (cont.)

❧ Choreography

Audiences can be mesmerized by dancers moving across the stage alone, in pairs, or in groups. Dancers seem to move seamlessly from individual locations as they join as a group and then part to return to individual spots. Choreographers orchestrate this motion through the planning and notation of movement.

Choreography requires students to decide how to incorporate movements, pathways, tempo, and location into a creative movement piece and then notate or communicate those decisions. Without such notation, dance instructions could not be transmitted over time (Waters and Gibbons 2004).

❧ Movement Phrases

In this strategy, students create a series of movements to represent the parts of a process or concept. They perform this series of movements, linking each to the next, to illustrate a series of steps or components within a curricular concept. When students link ideas, they can better understand relationships among concepts and form generalizations. As students create and build upon their movement ideas, they also develop the vocabulary of movement such as directional words (pathways), and levels (high, medium, low). According to Stacey Skoning (2008), "having a common movement vocabulary in the classroom benefits everyone because the common vocabulary makes it easier to discuss the movement phrases that are being created."

Embodiment

Model Lesson: Inferring Theme

Model Lesson Overview

In this strategy, students use embodiment to explore the themes they find throughout different texts in short movement responses. Students work in groups to physically explore and deepen their understanding of themes through movement, and they share their ideas with the class.

Standards

K–2

- Knows the theme of a story
- Moves his or her body in a variety of controlled ways
- Creates shapes at low, middle, and high levels

3–5

- Knows themes that recur across literary works
- Creates shapes at low, middle, and high levels
- Uses kinesthetic awareness, concentration, and focus in performing movement skills

6–8

- Understands inferred and recurring themes in literary works
- Understands various movements and their underlying principles

Materials

- Text of choice (picture book, novel, primary source photograph, song, painting, etc.)
- *Embodiment Brainstorming Guide* (page 30, embodimentguide.pdf)
- *Observing Others* (page 31, observingothers.pdf)

Embodiment *(cont.)*

Preparation

In the days and weeks leading up to this lesson, engage students in direct instruction on how to infer themes in a text. This can be accomplished during daily read-alouds by modeling how to infer themes as you read. Mark the page with the words that support your inference and discuss with students how to identify a theme in a text.

Think about what size student groupings would be most productive for creating these embodied representations. For this lesson, choose a picture book, section from a novel, oral history, etc., that portrays a theme. See Appendix C: Recommended Resources for suggested texts. Additional ideas are provided in the Specific Grade Level Ideas.

Procedure

1. Model embodiment with the whole class by playing "Answer Me In Movement." Tell students that you are going to name a theme from a text that they have read, such as overcoming fear. Say, "As I introduce each idea, show me how you understand the concept through movement." You might say, "Overcoming fear," and then say, "Answer me in movement." Students should respond by using their bodies to create shapes and movements that express their understanding. Encourage students to use low, middle, and high levels of space to make their shapes and movements more interesting and to show different directions through the lines of their bodies.

2. Read aloud the picture book or section from the novel you chose. Then, distribute the *Embodiment Brainstorming Guide* (page 30) to students. Have them brainstorm theme(s) they find in the text, evidence from the text that reveals the theme(s), and ways to represent the theme(s) through brief creative movement responses. Record responses for students to reference throughout the lesson.

3. Have students break into small groups and choose one of the themes from the *Embodiment Brainstorming Guide* to show in movement as a group. Encourage students to choose a theme that they find challenging to remember or would like to understand more fully. Tell groups that they should not share their chosen theme outside their group so that when they present their movement, classmates can try to identify the concept being represented while describing the characteristics of what they see being depicted in the movement.

4. Using the Planning Questions, ask students to discuss their themes and ideas for movement. Instruct students to turn their ideas into movements and gestures that symbolize the main ideas from the text. Encourage students to focus on qualities of their ideas instead of trying to act out a scene from the book.

Embodiment *(cont.)*

5. As students work, check in with each group to provide encouragement and ask questions to deepen conceptual development. In some cases, students may use a symbolic gesture such as holding hands to show the theme of friendship. Encourage students to move beyond iconic symbols (e.g., peace symbols shown by holding two fingers up) and explore the meaning of the idea in inventive ways through movement.

6. Have each group present their embodiment to the rest of the class twice so that the audience has time to take in the details. Viewers can record their observations by using *Observing Others* (page 31). Ask viewing students to use their observations to identify the theme being represented. Use viewer observations as a catalyst to spark conversations about the ideas represented.

7. Use the Questions for Discussion to prompt students' reflections on how they translated ideas into movement and what they saw in other groups' embodiments that suggested a particular theme.

Planning Questions

- What moments in the story do you remember that suggested this particular theme?

- How might you show a particular theme with your body?

- What qualities in the theme will be important to share (emotions, big ideas, etc.)?

- How might you boil down the essence of an idea into a gesture or embodied movement that represents the qualities of the idea?

Questions for Discussion

- How did you translate the theme into movement?

- What choices did you make in creating movement?

- In what ways did movement help you understand a theme?

- What was the experience of embodiment like for you?

- Which themes were challenging to embody?

- What struck you about other groups' presentations?

- What themes do the movements seem to represent?

- What similarities and differences were there in the different movements of the same theme?

- How did this exploration change or deepen your understanding of theme?

Embodiment *(cont.)*

Specific Grade Level Ideas

K–2

Gather a set of texts that have familiar themes, such as fear, friendship, family, or love for animals. Sources may include songs, newspaper articles, interviews, or poetry. As a class, brainstorm a list of words that show feelings and possible gestures that they could use to show these feelings. In addition to exploring theme, this strategy can be used to examine the concepts of character or conflict.

3–5

In addition to the K–2 Specific Grade Level Ideas, encourage students to identify more than one theme in a text. Students can keep track of the themes as they find them and keep a list of titles that share similar themes. Students can delve deeply into social and cultural themes and examine how those same themes occur in books written during different time periods. In addition to exploring theme, this strategy can be used to examine the concepts of character or conflict.

6–8

Ask students to connect the themes of a historical fiction text with the true events of its time period. Encourage students to explore a theme through a wide range of sources about the same topic, including historical documents, digital photographs, interviews, and oral histories from the Library of Congress website. Challenge students to show the significance of the times through embodiment. Ask students to consider how particular perspectives of a time period are represented in a text, such as fear, prejudice, or social class. Encourage students to use movement to explore more abstract ideas and qualities as opposed to literal representations of the story. In addition to exploring theme, this strategy can be used to examine the concepts of character or conflict.

Name _____ Date _____

Embodiment Brainstorming Guide

Directions: Use the chart to help you show themes through movement.

Theme	Evidence from the text	Movement Ideas

Name _____   Date _____

Observing Others

Directions: As you watch each group perform, record your observations and questions in the chart.

Group Members	What Movements Did You Observe?	What Themes Did the Movement Suggest? How/Why?	What Questions Do You Have for the Artists?

Interpretation

Model Lesson: Inferring a Character's Feelings

Model Lesson Overview

In this strategy, students listen to a story about a character who has strong feelings or feelings that change over time. In small groups, students use interpretation to infer a character's feelings and make personal connections in order to understand him or her. Then, they use movement to communicate their interpretations.

Standards

K–2

- Knows the main characters in a story
- Relates story events to personal experiences
- Creates shapes at low, middle, and high levels

3–5

- Understands elements of character development in literary works
- Makes connections between events in literary work and events in his/ her own life
- Knows how ideas are communicated through movement elements
- Knows basic actions and movement elements and how they communicate ideas

6–8

- Understands elements of character development
- Compares text events with his/her own and other readers' experiences
- Understands various movements and their underlying principles

9–12

- Understands the elements of character development
- Identifies and demonstrates movement elements and skills

Materials

- Book that explores a main character's feelings or how a main character's feelings change over time
- *Movement Ideas* (page 36, movementideas.pdf)
- *Character's Feelings* (page 37, feelings.pdf)

Interpretation *(cont.)*

Preparation

Select a book that will inspire an examination of a character's feelings or how those feelings change over time, such as *I'm in Charge of Celebrations* by Byrd Baylor, *The Rag Coat* by Lauren Mills, or *How Many Days to America? A Thanksgiving Story* by Eve Bunting. If possible, gather multiple copies of the book so that small groups can carefully examine the text. Review *Movement Ideas* (page 36) in order to consider possible movements that express feelings, choices, and emotion. Additional ideas are provided in the Specific Grade Level Ideas.

Procedure

1. Activate students' prior knowledge about character by asking questions such as, "How do we know how a character is feeling? What causes characters to change throughout a text?"

2. Ask students how they can show a particular quality, trait, or emotion through movement. Work through an example together such as, "How can you show anger through movement? How would you describe the quality of the movement that depicts this emotion?"

3. Discuss with students different qualities of movement. For example, students can stay in one place and swing their arms (axial movement) or move through space. They can vary the speed and timing of their movements as well as the sharpness or fluidity. They can use their bodies to make shapes at different levels (low, medium, or high) and/or make pathways.

4. As a class, practice creating interpretive movements by working through the emotions of anger, bliss, and hopelessness, and have students play with movement ideas and describe what kinds of movement captures the essence of each emotion. Distribute *Movement Ideas* (page 36) to students and have them develop a bank of movement ideas they can work from as they move forward.

5. Read aloud your chosen book featuring a main character who has strong feelings or whose feelings change over time. Ask students to point out specific places in the text where they can infer the main character's feelings.

6. Explain to students that they will work in small groups to explore how the character is feeling and how his or her feelings change over time by using interpretation with movement. Encourage students to work with qualities of feelings as opposed to literal pictures of an emotion. For example, instead of showing someone crying, one might show a sinking feeling by lowering one's body slowly to the ground.

Interpretation *(cont.)*

7. As a class, record a list of events from the story and the character's emotions during those events for students to reference throughout the lesson. Divide students into groups according to the different events/feelings the character experiences over time.

8. Distribute *Character's Feelings* (page 37) to students. Have groups complete the activity sheet for their event/feeling and create interpretive movements.

9. Allow time for students to practice their movement. Then, invite groups to perform their interpretations of a main character's feelings throughout the text through movement.

10. Gather the class and reflect on the process, using the Questions for Discussion.

Questions for Discussion

- How did movement help you to explore what the character experienced and how it made him or her feel?

- How did interpretation help you understand a character's feelings and how they changed?

- What did you notice about the shifts in emotion portrayed as students performed their work?

- Describe the movement qualities you observed that showed particular emotions.

- How did you recognize a particular emotion?

Specific Grade Level Ideas

K–2

Complete *Movement Ideas* as a class, using drawings instead of words to depict students' ideas, if needed.

In addition to character, the concepts of theme and problem/resolution can be explored using this strategy.

Interpretation *(cont.)*

3–5

As an extension, invite students to think about experiences and feelings from their own lives. Students can explore movements to communicate the feelings associated with these memories.

In addition to character, have students explore the concepts of theme, conflict/resolution, and cause-and-effect using this strategy.

6–8

Have students complete *Movement Ideas* independently and then share their ideas in small groups before working on their assigned event/emotion.

As an extension, invite students to examine the feelings communicated in their own personal writing and create interpretive movements to explore those further. Students can then use the experience of movement as a tool to inform their writing in the process of revision. The concepts of theme, cause-and-effect, and point of view can also be examined using this strategy.

9–12

More complex novels with sophisticated character development can be used with these students. Students can also be assigned two corresponding events to interpret through movement in order to showcase through movement how the character's feelings change over time.

The concepts of conflict/resolution, cause-and-effect, theme, and archetypes can also be explored using this strategy.

Name _____ Date _____

Movement Ideas

Directions: Describe or draw movement ideas that embody the qualities of each emotion.

Emotions	Movement Descriptions
Anger	
Fear	
Love	
Worry	
Bliss	
Other:	
Other:	

Name _____   Date _____

Character's Feelings

Directions: Use the space provided to answer the questions with your small group.

What event did the main character experience? How did it make him or her feel? How do you know?

In what ways can you connect to how the character feels? What does this event remind you of?

Sketch or write about how you would express the character's feelings through movement.

Moving Statues

Model Lesson: Strong Verbs

Model Lesson Overview

In this strategy, students read a text with strong verbs. After an initial read for enjoyment, half of the class explores the qualities of movement words and phrases while the other half observes the movement. Then, groups switch roles. A final read of the text invites all students to enact moving statues when they hear the movement words.

Standards

K-2

- Understands words for actions
- Shows control over body movements
- Creates shapes at low, middle, and high levels

3-5

- Understands level-appropriate reading vocabulary
- Identifies and demonstrates movement elements and skills
- Creates shapes at low, middle, and high levels

6-8

- Understands an author uses word choice to accomplish his or her purpose
- Reproduces simple movement sequences

Materials

- Book that features strong verbs
- *Movement Words and Phrases* (page 42, wordsandphrases.pdf)

Preparation

Select a book that features strong verbs, such as *Song for the Whooping Crane* by Eileen Spinelli, *Flip, Float, Fly: Seeds on the Move* by Joann Early Macken, or *Tiny Little Fly* by Michael Rosen. Additional ideas are provided in the Specific Grade Level Ideas.

Moving Statues *(cont.)*

Procedure

1. Review the word *verb* and how a verb shows action. Explain to students that they will examine how the author uses strong verbs so that the reader can picture precisely what the characters are doing and the qualities and characteristics of how they are moving.

2. Read aloud the chosen text with strong verbs and rich figurative language. Encourage students to make mental images as you read.

3. Focus on a sentence from the text that has a strong verb. Ask students to tell you what they picture when they hear the strong verb. What if the author chose to use another verb? Would they be able to picture exactly what was going on?

4. Ask a student volunteer to use movement to demonstrate the verb.

5. Explain to students that they will enact moving statues as a way to more deeply understand the meaning of strong verbs and phrases. Model a moving statue with a phrase from the text that includes a strong verb by telling students to begin as a frozen statue. Then, when they hear the verb or verb phrase, they activate into movement that demonstrates it. Finally, they return to a frozen statue when they hear a clap. Note that beginning and ending with a still image will highlight the qualities of movement.

6. Tell students that they will choose some strong verbs and verb phrases to act out. Distribute *Movement Words and Phrases* (page 42) to students and read the text aloud again as students record the strong verb phrases they hear in the first column of the chart.

7. Have the class practice creating moving statues with the verbs and verb phrases they record. Remind students that everyone's movements could be different. Ask for a volunteer to read one of the verbs while the rest of the class is frozen as statues. Students should enact their movements once the verb/phrase is read. Have another volunteer read a second verb/phrase and repeat for practice.

8. Divide the class into two groups. One group will read the strong verbs/phrases they recorded, and the other group will create moving statues. The first group observes the second group's movements. Have groups switch roles halfway through.

9. If desired, read the book one more time. During this final read, all students move when they hear the action verbs and figurative language.

Moving Statues *(cont.)*

10. Debrief with students, using the Questions for Discussion to facilitate students' thinking about the process of creating moving statues. Record students' words describing movement.

Questions for Discussion

- What different movements did you make to represent the verbs?

- What did you observe about the movement of the verbs as you were watching others share their movement ideas?

- How would you describe the movement used to depict the verbs? What were the qualities of the movement?

- In what ways did movement help you understand the content?

- What did you find most challenging? Why?

Specific Grade Level Ideas

K–2

To brainstorm a variety of movements, invite students to close their eyes and slowly move their arms in interesting ways while staying in the same place. After a minute or so, have students open their eyes and brainstorm and record a list of verbs to describe their movements, such as *raise*, *lower*, *bend*, *point*, *circle*, *swing*, and *stretch*. Ask them to demonstrate these movements by using different parts of their bodies. For example, show how they might point with their pinkies, their legs, or their torsos. These words can be used in future movement work to spark ideas. Also, instead of having students complete *Movement Words and Phrases*, you could record strong verb phrases on sentence strips for students to reread and create a moving statue.

Moving Statues *(cont.)*

3–5

Extend this lesson by further exploring each verb: as a class, brainstorm a list of similar verbs with slightly different meanings. Invite students to use moving statues to demonstrate the slight variance of meaning. If desired, have students use a thesaurus or online dictionary to look up synonyms. For example, students can explore the differing but related meanings of *leap*, such as *skip* and *spring*, or the related versions of *wade*, such as *bathe* and *swim*. Additionally, students can explore antonyms. Also consider how incorporating different movement choices may yield a different list of verbs. Tracking and discussing these variations can develop students' abilities to understand and describe the characteristics of the movement, using precise and descriptive language.

After the exploration, have students revisit a writing piece that they are working on. Ask them to highlight the verbs they used and challenge them to replace everyday verbs with strong verbs.

6–8

In addition to the 3–5 Specific Grade Level Ideas, have students work in small groups to analyze the chosen text for other types of words the author uses to convey meaning and create moving statues for those ideas. In addition to exploring verbs and word choice, students can also create a fluid, whole-class moving statue in which students are moving to show how a character changes over time, the order of events in a story, or different moments in the text that show a theme. Students can also explore cause-and-effect relationships through moving statues in which half of the class represents a cause through movement and the other half represents the effect through movement.

Name _____ Date _____

Movement Words and Phrases

Directions: Use the chart to think of movement ideas for strong verbs.

Verbs	Movement Ideas

 #51090—*Strategies to Integrate the Arts in Language Arts*

Choreography

Model Lesson: Life Cycle Books

Model Lesson Overview

Students plan or *choreograph* a sequence of creative movements, focusing on living things in the life cycle and the pathways they follow and represent that plan on paper. They can also consider tempo. As students present the movement planned, they gain a kinesthetic experience of the life cycle. In this lesson, students read and examine how different types of nonfiction texts depict the same information. Students can explore different kinds of texts within the nonfiction genre at all levels.

Standards

K-2

- Reads a variety of informational books

- Understands the main idea and supporting details of simple expository information

- Uses locomotor movements in different directions

- Uses movements in straight and curved pathways

3-5

- Reads a variety of informational books

- Uses text organizers (e.g., headings, topic and summary sentences, graphic features, typeface, chapter titles) to determine the main ideas and to locate information in a text

- Uses locomotor movements in different directions

- Uses movements in straight and curved pathways

6-8

- Knows the defining structural characteristics and features used in informational texts

- Memorizes and reproduces movement sequences

Materials

- Various books about the life cycle

- *Pathways* (page 50, pathways.pdf)

- *Choreography Planner* (pages 48–49, choreographyplanner.pdf)

Choreography *(cont.)*

Preparation

Select life cycle books that depict the topic in different ways, including picture books in the narrative form and more traditional informational texts with graphic features. It is recommended to include at least one narrative nonfiction picture book and one traditional expository picture book. Some suggested titles include *Monarch and Milkweed* by Helen Frost, *A Grand Old Tree* by Mary Newell DePalma, and *The Life Cycle of an Emperor Penguin* by Bobbie Kalman. See Appendix C: Recommended Resources for suggested texts.

Think about how students will best work together. To encourage all students to be involved in the problem-solving process, the planning and designing of choreography is best completed in groups of two to four students.

You will want to use an open meeting area, create an open space in the classroom, or plan to use another open space such as the gym or the cafeteria for the creative movement presentations. Additional ideas are provided in the Specific Grade Level Ideas.

Procedure

1. Begin by posing the questions "What is a life cycle?" and "What are examples of a life cycle?" Share two different types of nonfiction books about life cycles, such as a picture book and an informational text with graphic features. Point out the stages of the life cycle and discuss with students the circular order of events. As a class, discuss the characteristics for each type of life cycle book. What features do the two texts have in common? How do they share facts in different ways? Let students share opinions about which texts they prefer. Which type of text is easier for students to read and understand? Why might an author choose to depict information in such different ways?

2. Display the term *pathway* and define it as the path a movement or combination of movements can take. Distribute *Pathways* (page 50) to students, which illustrates five possible movement paths: *straight*, *zigzag*, *curve*, *spiral*, and *circle*. Have students stand up and explore making a variety of movements along the different pathways.

3. Divide students into groups. Ask groups to explore movement ideas for each stage of the cycle shown in the different style of books. Have them show the features of that stage through movement. Tell students that they may choose to show the stages as a narrative (like a picture book) or in a more informative way (like a nonfiction book with charts or graphs). Invite each group to share with the class their favorite movement idea for each stage in the order of the cycle. This will help students learn from one another and gather ideas for their own choreography.

Choreography *(cont.)*

4. Explain to students that *choreography* is the planning of movement sequences that combine to make a creative movement that hangs together. Divide students into groups again, but with different group members. Explain to students that each group is going to choreograph movement about life cycles using the information from their books. Have each group brainstorm ways to portray each life cycle phase through movement and how to connect each movement idea through movement transitions so that one stage flows into the next. Ask students to link their movement ideas until they have choreographed a creative movement piece that depicts the characteristics of their life cycle.

5. Distribute the *Choreography Planner* (pages 48–49) to students and have them answer the questions to help them choreograph their movement. Tell them to consider the pathways they will use in their movements and to make notes about those as well. Use the Planning Questions to help students plan their choreography. Allow time for groups to create and rehearse their choreography.

6. Invite groups to perform their choreographed work for the class. Debrief using the Questions for Discussion, focusing on how the features of the texts aided students in choreographing their pieces.

Planning Questions

- How can movement be used to show the changing phases of the cycle?

- How can you show how one phase evolves into the next through movement?

- How will your movers start and end their piece?

- What pathways will you follow?

- How can you add heightened interest to the choreography?

Questions for Discussion

- What was similar and different about the choreographies?

- What artistic choices were made by each group to depict different stages?

- What are the characteristics of a life cycle book written as a picture storybook? How did these features influence the choreography?

- What are the characteristics of a life cycle book written as a chart-based traditional text? How did these features influence the choreography?

- Why is it important to know what type of nonfiction you are reading?

- What did you notice about the features of each phase of the cycle in watching the creative movement choreographies of others?

Choreography *(cont.)*

Specific Grade Level Ideas

K–2

Kindergarten students can explore the activity as written without using the reproducibles. You can also use this strategy to have students conduct different kinds of genre studies. First- and second-grade students can learn about biographical or historical texts that are organized in a chronological order. They can choreograph concepts from the texts and then practice performing the movements in the correct order.

Gather nonfiction concept books about topics such as colors, the alphabet, or any related content appropriate for students. Invite students to create their own concept books, using the collection as mentor texts. Then, use specific ideas from particular concepts and ask students to create movements that can be linked together into a choreography.

3–5

Have students use a nonfiction book as a mentor text to write their own life cycle books. They can include nonfiction graphic features such as diagrams, photographs, or flow charts. Students should study the writer's craft involved in creating a life cycle book in the form of a story and write their own.

Encourage students to think about movement as another language for sharing information, much in the same way that nonfiction graphic features complement, deepen, or more fully represent ideas offered in a text. Students can experiment with noting movement choices within their choreographed work, comparing and contrasting how the embodiment of ideas compares or contrasts with information shared through text, image, diagram, or charts.

Students' choreography plans can indicate a variety of pathways as well as locations. They can also indicate the order in which the movers join or leave a group.

Choreography *(cont.)*

6–8

In addition to the 3–5 Specific Grade Level Ideas, students can explore how a life cycle book compares and contrasts with other subgenres of nonfiction literature such as survey books, biographies, and specialized nonfiction. Ask students to determine the purpose of each subgenre and how it communicates messages to the reader. Movement can be used to compare and contrast the qualities of each subgenre or to explore the main ideas in a text. Each mover can work with multiple pathways in the development of their movement sequence.

Name _____ Date _____

Choreography Planner

Directions: Use the questions to help plan your choreography.

1. What qualities and processes of the life cycle will your choreography show?

   _____

   _____

2. Where will your movers start?

   _____

   _____

3. What pathways will they follow?

   _____

   _____

4. What creative movement choices will you ask your movers to perform as they move along pathways?

   _____

   _____

5. How will they move along the pathways?

   _____

   _____

Choreography Planner *(cont.)*

6. What will the relationship be between movers?

_____

_____

7. What transitions will occur during the piece?

_____

_____

8. What shapes will movers make to begin the creative movement?

_____

_____

9. What notes should you add to your plan?

_____

_____

10. How could you add heightened interest to the presentation?

_____

_____

Name _____ Date _____

Pathways

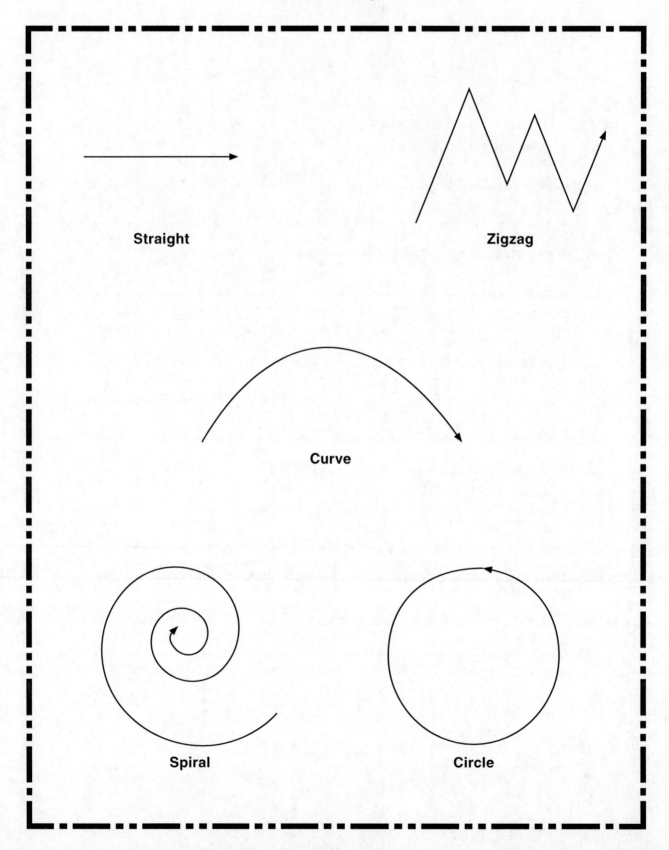

Straight

Zigzag

Curve

Spiral

Circle

Movement Phrases

Model Lesson: Plot

Model Lesson Overview

Students explore the plot of a realistic fiction story by linking movements to form movement phrases that explore complex events. Groups focus on the qualities of movement and movement transitions between ideas as they represent the following elements of plot: *exposition*, *rising action*, *turning point*, *falling action*, and *resolution*. The groups then work together to perform their movement phrases in sequential order. Note that students are exploring the characteristics of these literary ideas through movement rather than "acting out" the specific story. Students also focus on the qualities of movement such as *sustained*, *swing*, *percussive*, and *collapse*.

Standards

K-2

- Understands the sequence of a story
- Knows the main events in a story
- Creates a dance phrase, repeats it, and varies it

3-5

- Understands the basic concept of plot
- Uses locomotor movements in different directions
- Creates a dance phrase, repeats it, and varies it

6-8

- Understands complex elements of plot development
- Understands choreographic principles, processes, and structures

9-12

- Analyzes the use of complex elements of plot in specific literary works
- Understands choreographic principles, processes, and structures

Materials

- Realistic fiction text
- *Six Qualities of Movement Reference Sheet* (pages 56–57, qualitiesmovement.pdf)
- *Movement Phrase Graphic Organizer* (page 58, movementgo.pdf)

Movement Phrases *(cont.)*

Preparation

Select a realistic fiction text. Students should be familiar with the characteristics of the genre of realistic fiction. Identify how many students will work together to create a movement phrase. Read the *Six Qualities of Movement Reference Sheet* (pages 56–57) to become familiar with these descriptions of movement. Additional ideas are provided in the Specific Grade Level Ideas.

Procedure

1. Ask students how they link ideas in their writing. Record responses for students to reference throughout the lesson. Talk about the importance of giving examples and connecting ideas. Explain to students that when we connect movements, we create movement phrases and that such sequences can describe and represent the essence of a literary idea or story.

2. Share a realistic fiction story with students and discuss the characteristics of the genre. Review the elements of plot appropriate to your grade level. Tell students that they will explore the plot of the realistic story by creating movement phrases.

3. Divide students into small groups. Ask students to talk in their groups about how they could represent the sequence of the plot through creative movement. Remind students to think conceptually rather than creating a literal acting-out of ideas. Have groups share their thinking with the class. Record their ideas to generate a class list of movement choices that can be used to create their movement phrase and referenced throughout the lesson.

4. Distribute the *Six Qualities of Movement Reference Sheet* (pages 56–57) and review the ideas with students. Note that the goal is not to have students memorize this list but to offer them new ways to think about how a movement is performed and thus communicated in nuanced ways. Allow time for students to investigate some of the movements they have identified in their discussion, applying different movement qualities to them. For example, students might show a character metaphorically looking back over his or her life by turning their heads and looking back over their shoulder in a sustained slow motion. Have students explore different combinations of movements and qualities and take notes about those they found worked well together.

5. Distribute the *Movement Phrase Graphic Organizer* (page 58) and explain to students that they will use it to summarize their thinking. Have students work in their groups to identify at least three components or steps they will represent in their movement phrase along with the plot ideas, movements, and movement qualities to be used. Multiple copies of this graphic organizer may be needed for each student depending on the number of plot elements being analyzed.

Movement Phrases *(cont.)*

6. Encourage students to explore different combinations of movements before they make final choices. Use the Planning Questions to guide their thinking.

7. Ask students to discuss and then indicate the sequence of the components in their movement phrases by numbering them on the organizer.

8. Tell students to identify how they will use creative movement to transition from one component to the next. Students should record these decisions for their own reference.

9. Allow time for students to explore their choices physically and to rehearse their phrase until they are ready to present it to the whole class.

10. Have groups present their pieces. Ask students to begin and end in stillness in order to heighten the awareness of the movement.

11. Have viewers observe the movement presentations closely and identify the ideas being portrayed as well as the movement choices that were most compelling. Use the Questions for Discussion to prompt students' reflections on their process of translating ideas into movement and what viewers saw in the movement phrase that suggested the ideas in the plot that were interesting to watch.

Planning Questions

- How will your creative movement choices communicate ideas about the plot?

- What might this look like as ideas are linked together in a sequence?

- How can you connect these ideas together in smooth transitions so that one movement idea flows into the next?

- How does your movement sequence communicate like a sentence?

- How might you vary your movement choices to heighten interest?

Questions for Discussion

- In what ways did movement phrases help you focus on one element of the plot?

- What did you learn about plot elements during the process of translating ideas into movement?

- What choices did your group make in the creation of the movement phrase?

- What struck you about the creative movement choices in the work as it was shared?

- How did movement phrases help you understand the different aspects of plot?

- How did movement phrases help you understand cause-and-effect relationships?

- How might the ideas in the movement phrases allow you to experience the story more fully?

Movement Phrases (cont.)

Specific Grade Level Ideas

K–2

Students can use movement phrases to focus on the qualities of a sequential plot, specifically representing the beginning, middle, and end of the story. Have students determine the information that authors typically include in those sections of the story and how that helps to move the story forward.

Depending on where your students are developmentally, you may also choose not to include the quality of movements in the procedure or only introduce a couple of them by modeling.

For first- and second-grade students, have them use movement phrases to represent the plot in stories they have written. Have them use the experience with movement phrases to revise their stories to include elements of plot.

3–5

In general, students can follow the procedure as written. Take time to review the terms on the *Six Qualities of Movement Reference Sheet* to increase students' confidence with the vocabulary.

Once students have explored the plot of a story through movement, invite them to begin collecting ideas to write a realistic fiction story of their own. Have them brainstorm ideas about what a character may want or a challenge he or she may have to overcome. Have students show the plot of their own fiction stories through movement phrases. Have them use the experience of movement to revise their written work.

Movement Phrases (cont.)

6–8

Students can use movement phrases to focus on more sophisticated elements of plot, such as cause-and-effect relationships, subplots, and parallel episodes in the texts they are reading.

Have students write their own realistic fiction stories and represent the plot in small groups through movement phrases. Have them use what they learned from the movement experience as a tool for revising.

9–12

Students can create movement phrases to represent other elements of a story, such as character traits and how characters interact with one another. Movement phrases can also show how characters transform throughout the plot of a story or how character behavior is related to the sequence of the elements of the plot.

Six Qualities of Movement Reference Sheet

Percussive:

Percussive movements are quick, forceful, and sudden. They are broken up by quick pauses. Think of someone suddenly stomping his or her feet and pausing briefly afterward to increase the impact of the movement.

Sustained:

Sustained movements are flowing, ongoing, and smooth. Think of sliding your foot out away from your body in a long, fluid push.

Vibratory:

Vibratory movements are similar to percussive ones, but they are quicker and less forceful. The movements could involve tapping or shaking.

Six Qualities of Movement
Reference Sheet *(cont.)*

Suspension:

A suspension movement is the slight pause that occurs between motions. The pause can draw attention to the movement just before or after.

Collapse:

Collapse movements give in to the pull of gravity. They can be sudden movements, such as a quick fall to the floor, or they can be gradual motions, such as the controlled lowering of your leg.

Swing/Pendular:

A swing or pendular movement goes back and forth. An example would be an arm that swings up high, pauses briefly, and then returns back down.

Name _____ Date _____

Movement Phrase Graphic Organizer

Directions: Use this organizer as a place to brainstorm and develop ideas.

Idea # _____

Element of plot to be explored:	
Movement ideas	Qualities to be incorporated

Idea # _____

Element of plot to be explored:	
Movement ideas	Qualities to be incorporated

Idea # _____

Element of plot to be explored:	
Movement ideas	Qualities to be incorporated

Drama

Drama

Understanding Drama

Integrating drama into the language arts classroom can deepen students' connection with language arts concepts and foster students' ability to find relevance to their own lives and interests. Drama can provide engaging contexts for exploring language arts ideas. By enacting scenes that connect to a language arts concept or skill, students can apply their learning in real-world settings.

When we integrate drama into the language arts classroom, we invite our students to consider particular situations in which language arts ideas are embedded. As students explore these scenarios, they uncover and deepen their language arts thinking, make personal connections to language arts, and recognize its real-world relevance. Christopher Andersen (2004) notes that drama has the ability to recreate the essential elements in the world; as such, drama can place language arts in authentic situations that make sense to students.

When students explore language arts through the lens of a character, they are called upon to imagine themselves working through processes, events, and dilemmas. In their roles, they must make choices, solve problems, translate concepts, and articulate ideas. This process requires students to explain, persuade, clarify, and negotiate their thinking (Elliott-Johns et al. 2012). As students investigate perspectives that are different from their own, they expand their worldviews and develop an awareness of their own. Such experiences help students clarify their thinking, understand different perspectives, and consider new strategies for solving problems.

Drama will provide your students with contexts that can ground their language arts investigations. And of course, through dramatic explorations, students learn about and develop skills in drama as well.

Many of these strategies incorporate process drama in which the teacher and students work together to explore a problem or situation without a script through improvisation (O'Neill 1995). This allows the drama to develop organically, with students' ideas and impulses leading the way. These drama strategies provide a rich context for language arts investigations where students imagine themselves in a variety of language arts situations. Exploring language arts ideas through dramatic scenarios creates motivation for students to participate eagerly in the exploration of ideas from multiple perspectives.

Drama (cont.)

Strategies for Drama

◊ Teacher-in-Role

In this strategy, the teacher takes on the role of a character to introduce a drama. Teachers can model the kind of work that they will ask students to do or set the stage for a dramatic scene. Either way, the strategy serves as an invitation for students to join in the dramatic work, to imagine, or to consider *what if?* There is a variety of ways that the teacher can create this role. For example, the teacher can portray a character in a book who presents his or her perspective, become a historical character who shares thoughts at a time when a key choice must be made that will have a significant impact on unfolding events, or introduce an investigation by depicting a character who shares the details of a scenario and asks others to participate as related characters. The allure of seeing their teacher willing to engage in the creation of a scene compels students to suspend their disbelief and join in the dramatic enactment.

◊ Tableaux

Sometimes called image theater or human sculpture, *tableau* is a French word meaning "frozen picture." It is a drama technique that allows for the exploration of an idea without movement or speaking. In this strategy, students use their bodies to create a shape or full picture to tell a story, represent a concept literally, or create a tangible representation of an abstract concept. Working with physical stance (low, medium, high), suggested relationships (body placement and eye contact), and a sense of action frozen in time allows students to explore ideas and provides a range of ways for students to share what they know about a concept. One person can create a frozen image or a group can work together to create an image. The process of creating group tableaux prompts discussion of the characteristics of what is being portrayed. The learning occurs in the process of translating ideas to physical representation. Tableaux can also be used as a way to gain entry into a complex idea or bigger project (Walker, Tabone, and Weltsek 2011).

Drama (cont.)

✂ Enacting Scenes

The bread and butter of drama is the development and enactment of scenes. Students portray characters that find themselves in particular settings and influenced by specific circumstances. They make choices, solve problems, and react to relationships with other characters. We watch (or participate) as characters make choices and deal with implications. Scenes are valuable thinking frames and can be used flexibly across content and contexts. Studies suggest that learning through drama benefits comprehension, including increased confidence with speaking, fluency, and working with complex language (Brouillette and Jennings 2010). Drama integration supports writing skills in terms of focus, use of details, and the navigation of meaning through the consideration of multiple perspectives (Cremin et al. 2006). Students can enter a suggested scene or create their own in response to a particular context, need, dilemma, or topic. They find that a story is enacted through a series of scenes.

This process of acting out a text provides a meaningful opportunity for students to go back through the text and reread parts that were not clear, visualize elements in the story, and consider character choices, the role of context, circumstance, and character motivation. Students imagine the character coming to life, question what they are reading, and check for story elements in a natural, purposeful manner. This metacognition, or being aware of the reading strategies as they are used, leads students to a deeper understanding of the text.

✂ Monologue

A *monologue* is a dramatic scene performed by one person. In creating a monologue, students take on the perspective of a character in a story, real or imagined, and speak directly to the audience for one to three minutes. The character must be established without interactions with others (that would be a dialogue) and must speak in a way that engages the audience with this singular focus.

There are often monologues in stories and plays that illuminate what a character is thinking. Most often, a monologue reveals a conflict of some kind that the character is wrestling with, a choice to be made, or a problem to be solved. Note that variations include *soliloquy* in which a character is speaking to him or herself. The creation of a monologue provides the opportunity to investigate what Barry Lane calls a "thoughtshot" of a character's inner thinking (1992).

This strategy allows students to "get into the head" of a particular character. Eventually, the goal is for students to create their own monologues, but you may want to introduce the strategy by having students explore prepared ones in resources such as *Magnificent Monologues for Kids 2: More Monologues for Every Occasion* by Chambers Stevens and *Minute Monologues for Kids* by Ruth Mae Roddy.

Drama *(cont.)*

❧ Monologue *(cont.)*

Then, students can develop characters and create and perform monologues for inanimate objects or forces, or they can portray specific characters (a historical figure, a character from a book, a newspaper article, a painting, or they can create an imagined character). In order for a monologue to be dramatic, the character must have some tension or conflict that he or she is wrestling with. This conflict can be an internal or external dilemma. Its resolution or the exploration of this tension will create dramatic interest

❧ Improvisation

A foundation of drama, improvisation is when individuals create a scene or dramatization "in the moment," making it up as they go. This kind of drama unfolds in exciting and often unpredictable ways as circumstances and character motivation come together to influence how a scene progresses. Improvisation can develop divergent thinking, language use, and social skills while allowing students to test ideas in a situation that is safe but feels real.

Teacher-in-Role

Model Lesson: Photographer's Snapshots with Words

Model Lesson Overview

The teacher invites students to imagine that they are photographers who are skilled at creating "snapshots," the detailed physical descriptions that allow readers to visualize a story's setting or character (Lane 1992). The teacher begins the scenario by "acting" as if he or she were a photographer who is introducing snapshots. This creates excitement and emphasizes the introduction, identification, and application of the writing strategy. The apprentice photographers (students in the class) gather and snap photographs (imaginary) and write snapshots about them. Though this exemplar focuses on photographers, you may vary your role from photographer to that of detective, designer, builder, conductor, or other roles that support a variety of content.

Standards

K–2

- Uses writing and other methods to describe familiar persons, places, objects, or experiences

- Uses descriptive words to convey basic ideas

- Understands the visual, aural, oral, and kinetic elements of dramatic performances

3–5

- Uses descriptive and precise language that clarifies and enhances ideas

- Understands the visual, aural, oral, and kinetic elements of dramatic performances

6–8

- Uses descriptive language that clarifies and enhances ideas

- Articulates the meanings constructed from one's own and others' dramatic performances

Materials

- *Sample Scenario* (pages 69–70, samplescenario.pdf)

- Photographer props (costume, camera, etc.)

- Descriptive excerpts from texts

- *Snapshots in Stories* (page 71, snapshots.pdf)

Teacher-in-Role *(cont.)*

Preparation

Review the *Sample Scenario* (pages 69–70) so that you are comfortable in the role. Adapt the script as needed for your students and area of focus. Note that you will be more convincing by improvising the role rather than reading from the script. Play with the tone of your voice to communicate emotion and slip into the role. You can make the activity more engaging by using a few props, such as a camera case, a tripod, and a notepad. Store these props out of sight before you launch the activity. Your willingness to be dramatic will intrigue students and help them to feel comfortable in taking their own dramatic risks.

Gather examples of descriptive excerpts from texts that you or students are currently reading. Alternatively, you may use the descriptions found on *Snapshots in Stories* (page 71). Additional ideas are provided in the Specific Grade Level Ideas.

Procedure

1. Tell students that you are going to begin a drama that invites them into an exploration of descriptive language and story. The idea is to have fun while bringing forward examples of descriptive writing from their own stories. Tell students that you will be introducing them to a photographer who is in town and would like to meet them.

2. Excuse yourself from the classroom for a moment and put on your photographer outfit. The scene begins when you say "Curtain up" and ends when you say "Curtain down." Say "Curtain up" before you enter, letting students know that the drama is about to begin, and reenter the room dressed as a photographer.

3. Begin the drama by clearly moving into the photographer role as you reenter the classroom. Adding a hat, glasses, or other costume elements will help students enter into the drama. Present the challenge to students, using the *Sample Scenario* (pages 69–70).

4. Invite students to go on a photo walk with you around the classroom, school, or schoolyard to use their (imaginary) cameras to take snapshots. Continue reading the script to carry out the lesson/drama as written.

5. Say "Curtain down" after the photo walk and after you have finished reading the script in order to alert students that the drama is ending.

6. Have students use the snapshot writing strategy to describe their imaginary photos. Tell students that writers use the snapshot strategy to help their readers create mental images of the characters or settings described in a story. Share examples of detailed descriptions from books you have read, or use the examples from *Snapshots in Stories* (page 71).

Teacher-in-Role *(cont.)*

7. Have students share the snapshots they wrote with partners or the whole class.

8. Push students' thinking by continuing the conversation in role using the Questions for Discussion. Note that the questions are also asked in role.

Questions for Discussion

During the drama:

- I see students taking snapshots of many familiar objects. Introduce your photographs to us by describing what you see in vivid language.

- I wonder if you could help me identify the best example of descriptive language from a story. What specific words allowed you to create a mental image?

- I am impressed by your abilities as photographers. Can you explain how you were effective in writing such descriptive language?

After the drama:

- How did participating in this drama set the stage for your exploration of snapshots?

- What did you notice about becoming a photographer? What did you notice about using your imagination as a tool for capturing an image?

Specific Grade Level Ideas

K–2

Following the lesson, students can write and share their snapshots with one another. As a class, create a symbol for students to use in their writing to indicate a place to add a snapshot. Ask students to locate two places in their writing, mark them with the symbol, and write snapshots.

Another way to extend this lesson is to have students work in pairs and share descriptive passages with their partners. Each partner draws a picture of the setting, scene, or action based on the descriptive words. Then, students discuss how accurate the pictures were based on the descriptions provided.

Teacher-in-Role *(cont.)*

3–5

Invite students to write letters (as apprentice photographers) to the photographer throughout the year and include specific snapshots from their work to celebrate their use of the snapshot strategy. In groups, students can use digital cameras or tablets to take pictures of scenes around the school building. Display the photographs and have students write snapshots from the images.

6–8

Students can find snapshots in songs, newspaper articles, magazines, podcasts, interviews, and oral histories found on the Library of Congress website. You can also engage students in creating dramatic representations of the snapshots that can be performed as the written snapshots are read aloud.

Sample Scenario

Curtain up.

(Act out an engaging entrance with camera in hand. Write Welcome, to the Photography Workshop! *on the board.)*

Well, hello, class! Did Mr(s). *(insert teacher's name)* tell you I'd be joining you this morning? I'm *(insert invented name)*, and I'm here to offer you a photography workshop. I'll be sharing some of my photographs with you and you'll be creating your own. Now, I should probably mention this is not just any camera. It's a snapshot camera. You'll notice that it requires a little more than film to make it work. You'll see what I mean in a moment.

Let's see, I think I brought a sample of my own photography. *(Dig around in a backpack, pretending to look for something. Then, pull out an imaginary photograph.)* Ah, here it is. I've blown it up big so you can really get a sense of it. Let me just take a second and post it so we can all experience it together. This is Ollie, my dog *(wave your hand toward the blank paper, acting as if there were an image.)* *(Pause.)*

Isn't he beautiful? What's the matter? Ah, you're thinking it's a photograph you can hold. No, no, no—I told you that it requires a little something more. It requires your imagination. Close your eyes and you'll see what I mean. Eyes closed? Okay, now, see if you can experience the photo.

(Read the following snapshot.)

My dog, Ollie, lay on his belly on the wood floor with a long, white bone in his mouth that he held tightly between his two front paws. His fur was curly and red except for the fur around his eyes and nose, which was white and rough and showed his age of 11 years. His eyes slowly scanned the room for potential bone thieves. SLURP, SLURP, SLURP was occasionally interrupted by joyful panting.

Okay, open your eyes. What did you notice about my snapshot? How do you think my snapshot came out? Did it create a clear and focused picture in your mind? What parts could you really see in your mind? Yes! You saw my snapshot. What else did you notice? Sounds?

Sample Scenario *(cont.)*

Now—let's see how you will do creating your own snapshots. I've brought a box of cameras. Where did they...? *(Look around as if searching for something.)* Ah yes—here they are. *(Walk over and pick up an imaginary box of cameras. Pretend to distribute them by holding the imagined box before each student until they pantomime taking one.)*

Go ahead, grab one—don't be shy now. Pick the color and size of the camera you like best. But hurry—we've got work to do. Come along. Let's go take some snapshots together. Bring your cameras!

(Take the class on a walk around the classroom, school, or schoolyard.)

Let's take a snapshot of this. *(Find object or scene to describe.)* Let me tell you how to use this camera. It's an older model where the film pops out once you've taken your photo, and you have to wait until it develops. You'll see the picture appear before your eyes. The interesting thing about this film is that it really captures all of the senses in it. Notice how you can see images, hear sounds, and even taste, feel, and smell. Truly! You'll see. Let's see what we can do. Everyone hold up your camera. Keep it steady. Be sure to really focus on the details you see and the sounds you hear. These cameras capture all of the senses. Okay, here we go, CLICK!

Who would like to share their snapshot with us? *(Ask students to use words to describe what they saw and heard. As guided practice, help craft their descriptions as needed. During this shared group snapshot, you can invite students to work together to build on each other's observation of sensory details.)* Wow! I can really picture these snapshots.

Let's head back to the classroom. *(Return to the classroom.)*

Now, I'd like each of you to write your own snapshot. Grab your writer's notebook. With a partner, take a picture with your camera. Then, show us the picture by writing a snapshot in your notebook. Include sensory descriptions, strong verbs, similes, or metaphors to help us picture it. When you're done, you will share it with your teacher. Hmmm, I'm not sure where your teacher went, but please show your teacher the excellent snapshots you've developed. I'll go see if I can locate your teacher. In the meantime, you get to work with your partner.

Curtain down.

Snapshots in Stories

Title of Book	Snapshot
Night Tree by Eve Bunting	"It hasn't snowed yet. It's so cold my breath hurts. The sky is spattered with stars, and the moon, big as a basketball, slides in and out between the treetops. Dad's lantern sweeps ahead."
Owl Moon by Jane Yolen	"It was late one winter night, long past my bedtime, when Pa and I went owling. There was no wind. The trees stood still as giants. And the moon was so bright the sky seemed to shine. Somewhere behind us a train whistle blew, long and low, like a sad, sad song."
The Buffalo Are Back by Jean Craighead George	"When the buffalo lived on the prairie, their sharp hooves helped rain reach deep into the earth, and the tough roots of the grass held in the wet. Now, no moisture remained in the soil. The farmer's crops withered and died."
Sarah, Plain and Tall by Patricia MacLachlan	"It was very quiet. The dogs leaned down to eat the hailstones. Seal stepped around them and leaped up on the fence to groom herself. A tree had blown over near the cow pond. And the wild roses were scattered on the ground, as if a wedding had come and gone there."
Grandma's Gift by Eric Velasquez	"Everyone was out in the streets shopping for food and gifts, and Grandma was ready to join them. So we dropped off my suitcase and headed straight to La Marqueta (the market)—one of my favorite places. This special group of shops and stalls sat under the elevated train tracks, and all the stalls rumbled and shook whenever a train passed overhead."
The Goat Lady by Jane Bregoli	"Cautiously, we picked our way through rocks and weeds toward her. The goats bleated to their owner between mouthfuls of hay. Around our feet chickens were busy pecking the ground for bits of grain the goats had dropped. The big gray goose came running toward us, honking a loud warning. We stood there bravely."

Tableaux

Model Lesson: Vocabulary Words

Model Lesson Overview

In this strategy, students use their bodies to create a tangible representation of an idea, vocabulary word, or concept. Working with level (low, medium, high), relationships (body placement and eye contact), and a sense of action frozen in time allows students to explore ideas and provides a range of ways for students to share what they know about a concept. Students create *tableaux*, or statues, to explore vocabulary words without moving or speaking. Once this lesson is modeled, teachers can extend the use of tableaux to encourage students to explore different vocabulary words found in their own texts in partners or as small-group work.

Standards

K–2

- Uses a picture dictionary to determine word meaning

- Understands level-appropriate sight words and vocabulary

- Knows various ways of staging classroom dramatizations

3–5

- Uses word reference materials to determine the meaning, pronunciation, and derivations of unknown words

- Understands level-appropriate reading vocabulary

- Knows various ways of staging classroom dramatizations

6–8

- Uses a variety of strategies to extend reading vocabulary

- Plans visual and aural elements for improvised and scripted scenes

9–12

- Extends general and specialized reading vocabulary

- Communicates directorial choices for improvised or scripted scenes

Materials

- Text excerpts that include select vocabulary words

- Print or digital dictionary

- *Gallery Walk Observation Sheet* (page 77, gallerywalk.pdf)

Tableaux *(cont.)*

Preparation

As you prepare to use this strategy to explore vocabulary terms, think about how to group students so that more complex ideas can be represented. For tableaux, some students will serve as the "sculptors" while other students are the molding "clay." Students can be asked to create a single sculpture or a group sculpture. Group sculptures can be used to illustrate relationships or more nuanced ideas. Select concepts and identify group size before beginning.

Select text excerpts that embody the meaning of a particular vocabulary word. For example, teach the word *courage* with *Courage* by Bernard Waber, or teach the word *hope* with *Hope Is an Open Heart* by Lauren Thompson. See Appendix C: Recommended Resources for suggested texts.

As this activity involves physical interaction, review respectful ways to work together and respect issues of space. Students may wish to sculpt the "clay" with words or by demonstrating the movement themselves. Additional ideas are provided in the Specific Grade Level Ideas.

Procedure

1. Introduce what a tableau is by inviting two students to join you. Dramatize being a sculptor as you "mold" their bodies into a shape. You could, for example, show a literal representation of a *triangle* by inviting one student to stand straight to form one side of the triangle and the other student to bend at the waist, and with outstretched arms, form the other two sides. Ask viewers to identify the term.

2. Then, explain how students could explore a more abstract idea, such as compassion, by sculpting a cluster of people standing and reaching out their arms to a figure on the floor. Have students talk about the differences between making literal and abstract images, between single and group images, and between having a sculptor role and using group decision making.

3. Assign students a vocabulary word to illustrate through tableaux. Decide if you want students to explore their own understanding of the word first or research it. As a class, use a dictionary (print or digital) to determine the meaning of the word. Read text excerpts containing the word so that students experience it in context. Then, describe how students will be grouped. You may:

   - Have students work in pairs, one as the sculptor and the other as clay. The sculptor molds clay into a human sculpture that represents the word.

   - Have students work in small groups. One or two group members go to the center of the room and begin the sculpture with a pose. The rest of the participants "add on" one by one to create a group sculpture until all group members are involved.

Tableaux *(cont.)*

- For more complex ideas, you may ask students to create a "slide show" in which they create multiple tableaux that show a progression. Images are presented one right after the other. The viewers can share their thinking about what they have seen following each slide show. The presenters can say "Curtain down" and "Curtain up" between images, indicating that the viewers should close their eyes in between slides so that they see only the still images and not the movement as images are formed.

4. Allow time for students to determine how to represent their vocabulary word through tableaux. Once students have developed their ideas, have them present their tableaux to the class. Introduce the presentations by saying, "Imagine we are in an art gallery. We'll walk around and look at the sculptures. At each stop on our gallery walk, we will talk about what we see and brainstorm what terms you think are being portrayed and how what you see in the tableau suggests the term." Distribute the *Gallery Walk Observation Sheet* (page 77) to students and say, "We'll use this to track the list of the words you use to describe what you see, and we'll find out from our sculptors what the term is and how our guesses relate to the concept represented in the tableaux."

5. Depending on the way the tableaux have developed, sculptors could demonstrate their forming of the clay or students could just get into formation. Be sure to provide time for students to review the tableaux. Use the Questions for Discussion to guide student thinking.

6. As you move around during the gallery walk, have students keep listing the words used to describe the tableaux. You may want to keep a record as well. You will end up with a rich list of adjectives, synonyms, and metaphors that will allow students to see the vocabulary word represented in new ways. Add to the list as each group describes their process of creating the tableau. This is often where ideas are translated and the richest realizations occur. Documenting students' language will reveal the connections they have made.

Questions for Discussion

For the viewers:

- What concept do you think is being represented?

- What words come to mind as you view the tableau?

- What do you see in the sculpture that suggested the vocabulary word?

- What action is suggested?

- What is most compelling about how the image is composed?

- What similarities and differences were there in the different sculptures of the same word or concept?

Tableaux *(cont.)*

For the participants:

- Describe your process for creating an image that captured the essence of the word.

- What was the sculpting experience like?

- Which words were easy to illustrate? Which words were more challenging?

- What was it like to join the tableau?

- What did the descriptions offered by the viewers of the tableaux reveal about the words being presented?

Specific Grade Level Ideas

K–2

Provide students with vocabulary or concepts that are more concrete. Challenge students by having them use their bodies to create emotions, actions, or structures.

Have the whole class explore a word together. Have students work in small groups to create a tableau for the chosen word and see how each group represents the word differently. Words such as *family* can generate rich discussion of the many forms a family can have.

3–5

Use vocabulary found in informational texts that can be used with this strategy. For example, through tableaux, have students explore vocabulary terms in a nonfiction narrative such as *The Wolves Are Back* by Jean Craighead George. Potential terms include *wilderness, silenced, tranquil, peace, yearned, marveled,* and *frightened*. These more conceptual words will yield a wide range of rich descriptions that have strong connections to the words as students describe what they see in the tableaux.

6–8

Have students choose an unknown word in a text they are reading and write the word on an index card. Have pairs or small groups select an index card and use tableaux to represent the word, first discussing and then researching as needed. During the gallery walk, ask students to infer what the vocabulary words might be.

Tableaux *(cont.)*

9–12

Assign or have students choose terms or concepts related to a unit on Greek and Latin roots. Students can choose a root and then represent various terms that include that root word. An example would be enacting related terms using the *bio-* (life) root, such as *biology, biography, biologist,* and *biosphere.*

Name _____ Date _____

Gallery Walk Observation Sheet

Directions: As you observe the tableaux, record your observations in the chart.

Observation Notes	Tableau 1	Tableau 2	Tableau 3
Words to describe the tableaux			
Notes from the "sculptor" and "clay" about the process			
Vocabulary word being represented			
What we've learned about the concept			

Enacting Scenes

Model Lesson: Using Reading Strategies

Model Lesson Overview

In this strategy, cooperative groups work together to act out one scene from a text of any genre. Students take on the roles of specific characters, ideas, or environmental elements and act out scenes, such as the beginning, the middle, and the end. Through this process, students use reading strategies such as rereading and scanning for clarification as they plan their enactment.

Standards

K–2

- Uses mental images based on pictures and print to aid in comprehension of text

- Knows how to interact in improvisations

3–5

- Monitors own reading strategies and makes modifications as needed

- Knows how to interact in improvisations

6–8

- Uses specific strategies to clear up confusing parts of a text

- Organizes rehearsals for improvised and scripted scenes

- Interacts as an invented character in improvised and scripted scenes

Materials

- Supplies to use as props

- Text of any genre for enacting (folktale, mystery, nonfiction narrative)

- *Drama Planner* (page 81, dramaplanner.pdf)

Preparation

Gather props or supplies from which students can make props. Choose a text that can be enacted by students, preferably one with characters, ideas, and events that are easy to work on in small groups. Also, decide whether you would like each group to enact a different text or different scenes from the same text. Additional ideas are provided in the Specific Grade Level Ideas.

Enacting Scenes *(cont.)*

Procedure

1. Tell students that they will be creating and enacting scenes from a story. Divide students into small groups and assign a text, or have them choose their own.

2. Explain to students that enacting a scene from a story will require close attention to detail in the text. Discuss the reading strategies that students will find themselves using as they prepare to enact their scene: rereading the text, scanning the text for important information, identifying actions that move the story forward, visualizing the characters and details of the setting, determining the author's message, considering story elements, visualizing scenes as they create a beginning and an end, and using any prior knowledge about the tale they may have.

3. Introduce the *Drama Planner* (page 81) and distribute a copy to each group. Provide time for students to work in small groups to read and reread the text. Monitor groups and point out reading strategies as you observe them being used or hear them being discussed. Are students rereading the text? Scanning for important information? Visualizing the characters? Considering story elements? Visualizing scenes as they create a beginning and an end?

4. Have students rehearse their scenes, improvising action and dialogue from what they remember about the story. Use the Planning Questions to guide students.

5. Have each group enact their scene for the class. After performing, have students write up their scenes in their writer's notebooks. Debrief with students about the process, using the Questions for Discussion. Highlight how their knowledge of the text (because of reading strategies that helped aid comprehension) contributed to a successful enactment.

Planning Questions

- How will you begin and end your scene?

- What props might you need to help dramatize the scene?

- What interesting action might take place as the plot unfolds?

- Besides the identified characters in the story, are there other objects or forces in the story that can be created as characters?

- What choices will you use in depicting your character (voice, movement, costume)?

- How will you show what your character wants in the scene?

Enacting Scenes (cont.)

Questions for Discussion

- What reading strategies did you use to draw upon information from the text in planning for your scenes?

- What other endings to your scene can you imagine?

- In what ways did enacting scenes affect your understanding of the text?

- What choices did you make in deciding how to enact your scene?

Specific Grade Level Ideas

K–2

Talk with students about the folktale about the Little Red Hen. If desired, read the book *Interrupting Chicken* by Ezra Stein and discuss how Little Red Hen changes the endings to the stories in order to save each character from an unfavorable outcome. Or discuss with students how they could change the original story in an unexpected way. Work with students to read and reread the story before enacting original beginnings and endings.

3–5

In addition to the K–2 Specific Grade Level Ideas, have groups create a scene that doesn't exist in the text but could. Have students improvise these scenes first and then write them in their journals and explain why these invented scenes would be meaningful to the text. You will find that the writing is more richly detailed and free flowing. Provide students with a digital camera to snap shots of particular moments. Students can tape these photographs into their writer's notebooks and write about the moment.

6–8

Have students choose a chapter from a book they are reading. Invite them to change the scene that happened before the chapter and to change the scene that happens after the chapter. Invite students to enact the scenes for the class. Note that you can take children's stories and adapt them for grade- and age-appropriate themes. For example, use *Interrupting Chicken* by Ezra Stein and discuss how Little Red Hen is an activist (she wants to make situations better for the main characters). Ask students to consider how they can change the outcome of the story if they were the authors and dramatize the new version. Can they create a story that mirrors themes from their lives?

Name _____   Date _____

Drama Planner

Directions: Work with your group members to plan the scene you will be enacting.

Story moment to be enacted: _____

_____

Characters involved in the scene: _____

_____

What does your character want in the scene? _____

_____

Action in the scene: _____

_____

Point of tension or conflict that triggers action in the scene: _____

_____

What reading strategies did you use to help you understand the story and plan your scene? Check off strategies from the list:

❑ I reread to remember or answer a question I had.

❑ I scanned for important information.

❑ I visualized the characters coming to life and details of the setting.

❑ I thought about the problem and solution.

❑ I determined the author's message.

❑ I used what I already knew about stories to understand my scene better.

Other: _____

Monologue

Model Lesson: Meet the Character

Model Lesson Overview

In this lesson, students use monologue to deeply understand a significant person or character after reading a variety of texts from a collection of books and primary sources (letters and quotations) and drawing from various modalities (print, audio, photographs, and artifacts). Using information from a variety of sources, students write and perform monologues in which they take on the perspective of a famous figure.

Standards

K–2

- Uses a variety of sources to gather information

- Uses variations of locomotor and nonlocomotor movement and vocal pitch, tempo, and tone for different characters

3–5

- Uses strategies to gather and record information for research topics

- Uses variations of locomotor and nonlocomotor movement and vocal pitch, tempo, and tone for different characters

6–8

- Uses a variety of resource materials to gather information for research topics

- Understands how descriptions, dialogue, and actions are used to discover, articulate, and justify character motivation

Materials

- Collection of texts about an individual or subject

- *My Notes* (page 88, mynotes.pdf)

- *Georgia O'Keeffe Monologue Sample 1* (page 86, monosample1.pdf)

- *Georgia O'Keeffe Monologue Sample 2* (page 87, monosample2.pdf)

- *Monologue Planner* (page 89, monoplanner.pdf)

Monologue *(cont.)*

Preparation

Gather a collection of texts that focus on the same person but are written by different authors. The collection might include biographies, historical fiction, poetry, articles, or primary sources. Draw from various modalities, including print, audio, photographs, and artifacts. Subjects could include artists (Georgia O'Keeffe, Pablo Picasso, Diego Rivera), historical figures (Rosa Parks, Thomas Jefferson, Marie Curie), animal activists (Jane Goodall), and conservationists (Rachel Carson). See Appendix C: Recommended Resources for suggested texts.

Read over *Georgia O'Keeffe Monologue Sample 1* (page 86) and *Georgia O'Keeffe Monologue Sample 2* (page 87) so that you can decide which is appropriate for your students. Present it to your students with dramatic interest. You may also select an example of a monologue from literature to share with students. Additional ideas are provided in the Specific Grade Level Ideas.

Procedure

1. Display the collection of texts and sources about your chosen individual or subject. Explain to students that when they look for texts about one subject, they will often come across different types of books—informational books and fictional books that sometimes include facts. They may also find poetry, articles, and primary sources such as letters and quotations. Talk to students about the importance of learning from those who have studied the individual or subject, such as authors, and, in the case of individuals, from the subjects themselves.

2. Introduce *My Notes* (page 88) to students and explain that they will be working in groups to read and analyze books about the same topic. Divide students into groups and distribute *My Notes* to each group. Circulate and facilitate group work as needed.

3. Once students have gathered notes on their topics, tell them that they will present the information they learned through monologue. Share *Georgia O'Keeffe Monologue Sample 1* (page 86) or *Georgia O'Keeffe Monologue Sample 2* (page 87) with students as a sample monologue. Talk with students about how a monologue is different from a dialogue.

4. Direct students to work in their groups, using the same books as reference material in planning a monologue. Distribute the *Monologue Planner* (page 89) to groups and have students work together to answer the questions and discuss possible ideas for a monologue.

5. Provide time for students to develop individual monologues in class. They should use their group notes and the texts as reference material. Then, have students present their monologues. Debrief the monologues using the Questions for Discussion.

Monologue (cont.)

Questions for Discussion

- What insights did you gain into the character by creating a monologue?

- What emotions did you feel as you experienced the monologue?

- What was your character's dilemma?

- In what ways does the character stay true to his or her ideals?

- How did using different types of texts and sources influence the way you created your monologue? How do you think it might have been different if you had only used one text?

Specific Grade Level Ideas

K–2

Use the *Georgia O'Keeffe Monologue Sample 1* with younger students. Students may find more success with this strategy when they are given a specific context—it helps them consider how their character would react in that situation. For example, ask them to imagine that they are entering a party where nobody knows their assigned character. How would they introduce themselves? What is important about their lives to share with others? Because conflict is the core of drama, ask students to focus on a dilemma that the character is trying to figure out. This can be a decision they have to make, a problem they have, or a turning point in a character's life.

Monologue can also be used to teach students about an author's purpose for writing and the genre they chose. Have students read different kinds of texts and create short monologues that explain why an author wrote a text in a certain way and what opinions that author holds about the topic.

Monologue *(cont.)*

3–5

Some students may choose to perform their monologues by putting on a show for invited guests. You can allow them to write their monologues on index cards so that memorizing the lines doesn't become more important than the exploration of character. Once students become deeply familiar with a character through rehearsing their monologue, they will be able to accurately improvise the piece. Having index cards available may help the performers relax as they share their work with the class.

Students can explore point of view, perspective, and motivation through the use of monologue. Have students read texts and then discuss them from various perspectives. For example, a fictitious historical account about the Revolutionary War can be discussed further by having students create opposing monologues—one from the point of view of a Revolutionary soldier and one from the point of view of a Loyalist colonist.

6–8

Have students create monologues from the points of view of other people and things in their character's life (e.g., Thomas Jefferson's pen, a flower in a Georgia O'Keeffe painting, the space shuttle Endeavour carrying Mae Jemison). Have them explore people from the same period in history or the same profession, and invite students to write a monologue from their points of view. Compare the character traits of these people through monologue. Explore the missing voices in a particular story or historical moment.

Students can also explore the way in which a monologue can fit into a longer dramatic performance. Students can consider and identify appropriate times for one character to speak in a scene that fits together with a multifaceted story.

Georgia O'Keeffe Monologue Sample 1

K–2

My approach to painting is different from what everyone else is doing. Moving against the crowd is hard! But I persist. I continue on because "I have things in my head that are not like what anyone taught me — shapes and ideas so near to me, so natural to my way of being and thinking." I cannot just walk by a flower without looking! Have you ever truly looked at a flower? I mean really looked at it? Come closer. Hold it in your hand. Now look. Look at the center. The way the lines branch out and create striking patterns. Notice the way the color is light in some places and dark in others….the way the contrast of light and dark make you want to look and look and look. "If you take a flower in your hand and really look at it, it's your world for a moment." Do you have things in your life that speak to you like this?

3–5

I always knew I was an artist. I remember walking the hills of Sun Prairie in the 1890s as a child and feeling drawn to rocks and plants in the beautiful Wisconsin landscapes. Even bones fascinated me. As I walked, something would capture my attention and I'd pick it up. I was drawn to it. Later, I'd sketch it. My parents and siblings were always telling me nature belongs outside and made me move my piles of treasures outside. I loved exploring the shape and color of a thing through color and line.

I took art lessons at home and drawing lessons from my grammar teacher. And my teachers in school encouraged me. But after high school I realized I wasn't good enough to make a career of painting realistically. I had attended the Art Students League in New York City in 1907 and I grew frustrated with my abilities. I felt for a time that I wasn't successful. I guess we all question ourselves along the way. I didn't want to work in traditional ways. And so, I stopped painting. I walked away from it. I destroyed every piece completed there. I was done with painting. I couldn't communicate in the traditional methods being used. I felt...stifled...like I couldn't breathe.

So, I felt lost for a time. I found other things to do of course instead of painting and life went on. I was a commercial artist for a while, I taught art in an elementary school. And then...one summer I took a course in art for teachers. And...everything changed. I connected with a professor who opened the world for me. Professor Arthur Wesley Dow was his name and he showed me that my art could be about feeling. About what was inside me. He encouraged me to work with light and dark color, and line. It was a moment for me...a turning point that seemed to snap things into focus in my life. I revisited my passion for nature. I believe the natural world has a deep power. The power of life in a flower, or a skull whitened by the sun is equal to the strength of a NYC skyline. Truly. It is.

I had found my true work.

Georgia O'Keeffe Monologue Sample 2

6–8

(Georgia O'Keeffe has a letter in her hand. She turns it over and reads the sender's address. She smiles slightly.)

The great photographer Alfred Stieglitz. Hmm, I wonder....

(Carefully she opens the letter and reads.)

Well, I'll be. One brief visit and he's reaching out. Good. My work has sparked his attention.

(She reads a quote from the letter.) "I can't stop thinking about your drawings and paintings. Your poppies, sunflowers, and jimsonweed. The blue Texas sky and lavender dawns. Ms. O'Keeffe, you intrigue me. You see the world in a way that is unique—through shape, color, and abstraction...."

(laughs) Too true, and I've been reprimanded for it all my life. How is it that you recognize my vision so quickly, so fully?

(She reads on.) "You must exhibit in New York. Won't you come? *(pausing)* Please consider it. I will raise the funding you need to paint full-time. Your work should be allowed to flourish. There's a whole new world for you here."

A whole new world. *(She looks out the window.)* Perhaps a whole new world is what's needed. I am well aware, Mr. Stieglitz, that I live in a time when society does not deem it proper for women to become artists. I've heard again and again that teaching art is not the proper place for a woman. "Women aren't meant to be artists!" Ridiculous! I have never followed the mainstream. But you see me. You understand my work.

I remember my first prize for an early painting I called *Dead Rabbit with Copper Pot*. I could feel the excitement coursing through my veins—the sense that this was my life unfolding. I have the same feeling now. My fingers are trembling. Alfred Stieglitz, he intrigues me. His style is distinctive. He's a pioneer, as I am. Though it's easier for a man these days to pursue his vision, he recognizes my view of the world.

All right, Stieglitz, I accept your invitation. *(She sighs with anticipation and looks into the distance.)* Georgia O'Keeffe in New York City.

Tonight, I'll sleep under the stars on the roof. Under the Texas sky I love so much. It will be hard to leave. The spirit of the land here inspires my work. The wind, the sky—there's no other place I feel so at home. Nature is my true company. But this Alfred Stieglitz. There is something about him....

(She gathers her things and strides confidently out of the room.)

Name _____ Date _____

My Notes

Directions: Brainstorm and develop ideas using the texts your group has been given.

Subject/individual being studied	
General background information	
Significant events (and feelings about these times)	
Conflicting information found in the texts	
Information learned from illustrations or photographs	
Other interesting facts (e.g., hopes, dreams, concerns)	

Name _____   Date _____

Monologue Planner

Directions: Answer the questions to help plan your monologue.

My character's name:	What has influenced your character?
Where does he or she live?	What are his or her values?
What is he or she known for?	What character traits does the character show? How?
What challenge, decision, or dilemma does the character have?	What does your character want in this monologue?

Improvisation

Model Lesson: Characters Come to Life

Model Lesson Overview

In this strategy, students identify character traits of specific characters based on evidence from texts and images and then improvise scenes based on their inferences of these traits. Students consider circumstance, relationship, and context as they enact how characters would behave, speak, and act in a particular situation.

Standards

K–2

- Uses pictures to aid comprehension about a character's behavior

- Plans and records improvisations based on literature

3–5

- Uses pictures to preview a text

- Plans and records improvisations based on literature

6–8

- Formulates ideas in response to a text

- Improvises, writes, and refines scripts based on personal experience and heritage, imagination, literature, and history

9–12

- Analyzes internal/external conflicts between main and subordinate characters

- Improvises, writes, and refines scripts based on personal experience and heritage, imagination, literature, and history

Materials

- Collection of wordless books

- *Getting Ready for Improvisation* (page 94, improvisation.pdf)

Preparation

Gather a collection of wordless books and review them before beginning this lesson. (*Note:* See suggested titles in Appendix C: Recommended Resources). Additional ideas are provided in the Specific Grade Level Ideas.

Improvisation *(cont.)*

Procedure

1. Provide students with time to browse the wordless books and learn about the genre. Encourage students to think about the following questions as they browse the books: Why do you think some authors choose to tell their stories through pictures instead of words? What information about the characters, settings, and story are revealed through illustrations? Are some events highlighted more than others? How? How do the authors reveal how the characters feel? How do the authors reveal the characters' traits?

2. Share a wordless picture book with the whole class, discussing the sequence of events as they unfold. Point out how the author uses body language and facial expressions to communicate the characters' thoughts and feelings. Tell them that when reading a wordless book, readers have to make inferences about the characters. These ideas are not revealed in words, so readers must make inferences based on the information provided by the pictures. Discuss the theme of the text: What is the message the author wants us to know?

3. Explain to students that one way to better understand what they read is to really get to know the characters by analyzing their traits and feelings. With students, brainstorm a list of character traits such as *persistent*, *responsible*, *courageous*, *honest*, and *innovative*. Brainstorm a list of words for feelings, such as *curious*, *anxious*, *hopeless*, *shocked*, or *frustrated*. Record responses for students to reference throughout the lesson.

4. Ask students to choose an interesting event in the book and explain why they have selected it. Select a student volunteer to help you model the use of improvisation to show what the character may be thinking or saying during this event. To do this, act out the scene and use words that come to mind based on what you know about the character's traits and feelings.

5. Distribute *Getting Ready for Improvisation* (page 94) to students. Have them work in pairs to choose one wordless book from the collection, complete the charts, and preplan their improvisation. Use the Planning Questions to stimulate students' thinking.

6. Invite partners to share their improvisations with the whole class. Discuss the improvisations, using the Questions for Discussion.

Improvisation *(cont.)*

Planning Questions

- What is happening in the scene?

- What can you infer about the characters from the information offered in the illustrations?

- What might the character be saying?

- What else do you know about the characters based on other things that are depicted in the story?

- How might you bring the scene to life through words and movement?

- How might you create your scene with a clear beginning, middle, and end?

- What is motivating the characters in the scene?

Questions for Discussion

- What choices were made that brought the story to life?

- What character traits were demonstrated through the improvisation?

- How did improvisation help you better understand the characters and how they respond to problems, setting, and plot?

- What did the improvisation tell you about the story and its characters that the book did not?

- How do the different motivations of characters drive the choices they make?

Specific Grade Level Ideas

K–2

Introduce students to the use of dialogue in order to deepen their improvisations, using a book that features dialogue, such as *Let's Play in the Forest* by Chris Rueda. Have students improvise a scene that occurs in the book or enact a variety of possible endings. Ask students to consider what is driving a character to act in the scene.

Improvisation *(cont.)*

3–5

In order to extend this lesson, have students create scenes that were not in the book but are referenced or suggested. Ask them to create new characters and to consider what characters or circumstances would shift the way that the plot unfolds and enact a variety of options. Once they are finished, students can document their improvisations in written form, noting the back-and-forth dialogue and description of action in their writer's notebooks.

6–8

Invite students to choose a character from a chapter book they are reading. Challenge them to give the character different motivations and to change certain circumstances in the text to see how the plot could unfold differently. This subtle shift requires students to remain true to their portrayal of a character, but what fuels character choices will have dramatic implications on how the scene unfolds. You could also give students slips of paper with different genres and ask them to perform the scene in the style of different genres (e.g., moving from comedy to tragedy).

9–12

Have students use improvisation to create a persuasive oral argument or a debate scenario between two or more characters. Provide students with questions or controversial statements and then ask them to improvise two or more "position statements" in character in order to support or defend one side of the argument or the other.

Name _____ Date _____

Getting Ready for Improvisation

Directions: Work with a partner to choose one of the following options. Take notes about ideas for action or dialogue for your characters.

Choose one scene from the book that you plan to act out. Write about or map the action that takes place in the scene.

Write words that come to mind as you think about what the character wants, what he or she is thinking, and, as a result, how the character feels and behaves.

Music

Music

Understanding Music

Music has played a significant role in every culture since the beginning of time. Due to recent technology, our favorite tunes are readily available to us, and music has become even more prevalent in our lives. Dr. Howard Gardner has identified musical intelligence as one form of intelligence (2011). His theory of multiple intelligence suggests that students learn in different ways, and for some students, connecting with rhythm, beat, and melody provides access to learning. And as any adult who has introduced a cleanup song knows, music can motivate children and help them make transitions from one activity to another. Recently, attention has been given to the benefits of music in academic performance. It has been suggested that early music training develops language skills, spatial relations, and memory (Perret and Fox 2006). Paquette and Rieg also note that incorporating music into the early childhood classroom is particularly beneficial to English language learners' literacy development (2008).

Gayla Kolb explores the natural relationship between music and literacy, noting that "the spontaneous disposition children have toward rhythm and melody makes music an ideal tool for assisting them with interwoven facets of language: listening, speaking, reading, and writing. Through music, children experience the wholeness of language" (1996).

In the strategies for this section, students explore language arts ideas alongside the basic elements of music. Students engage in singing, playing, and composing music as well as making an instrument. The focus is on deepening knowledge of language arts while experiencing the joy of creating music together in ways in which all students can participate. Along the way, students develop a deeper understanding of and skills in creating music. No previous musical training is needed for you or your students.

Exploring language arts through music engages and motivates students. As students identify, apply, and generalize ideas to real-world situations, language arts becomes meaningful and purposeful. Abstract ideas are connected to concrete models, and students' representational fluency deepens. The more avenues we provide for students to experience language arts, the more likely we are to connect with the variable ways in which students learn.

Music (cont.)

Strategies for Music

ଧ Found Sounds

Sounds are all around us; they are found when we attend to them or manipulate them. Think about the sound of light rain or the squeals of delight you hear near a playground. There is rhythm in these sounds. Composer R. Murray Schafer thinks about the world as a musical composition. He notes, "In [music] we try to get people to use their senses to listen carefully, to look carefully" (quoted in New 2009). What makes a sound music rather than noise may depend on the listener, but it is also related to pitch (high or low) and rhythm. When students collect found sounds, they gain a new appreciation for what music is and develop careful listening skills. They can also better understand the environment from which sounds come. Students can put sounds together in interesting compositions, exploring environment and contexts for where stories unfold, as well as the power of onomatopoeia as language mirrors sounds. Louise Pascale notes, "Often, we describe things visually rather than auditorially. Students can describe the sounds they find in a vivid way (e.g., a *loud* sound can become an *ear-piercing sound, brassy, shattering*, etc. This can build language" (Pascale, pers. comm. 2012).

ଧ Songwriting

When students sing, a deep connection is created with the melody, rhythm, and lyrics of a song. Further, creating and making music supports academic achievement (Deasy 2002). Though students have opportunities to sing in school, far less attention is given to their ability to create their own songs. This strategy invites students to become songwriters, and as they do so, they become more familiar with the importance of tone, rhythm, and beat. Students can begin on an intuitive level or simplify the task, for example, by creating new lyrics for a song they already know. This not only connects students to music but also to one another as singing together creates a sense of community. As songs can help us remember things, these adaptations can help students retain information from a variety of texts. Also, writing lyrics will prompt students to discuss, synthesize, and categorize curricular concepts. Students can explore rhythms on a drum or experiment with notes on a keyboard. As their musical knowledge expands, they can create original melodies as well as score their compositions.

Music (cont.)

Chants

Chants involve the rhythmic repetition of sounds or words. They can be sung or spoken. They can be a component of spiritual practices or heard on a football field. By combining different dynamics (ranging from soft to loud), pitch (variations from high to low), and different notes (length of duration), students can create engaging sound effects that help them learn and remember ideas. According to Dunn (1999), "a chant is a rhythmic group recitation." Chants can be used in a variety of ways. They can be created with catchy rhythms that make the associated words easy to learn and to remember. When this form of chants is emphasized, students retain important information related to language arts. Chants can also be constructed by layering phrases on top of each other that are then spoken or sung simultaneously. In this format, the use of differing rhythms and pitch create interest and suggest relationships among the chosen phrases and thus the content being considered. Chants allow for the exploration and observation of the natural rhythms of language.

Mash-Up

Mash-ups are the result of assembling parts of songs from a variety of music to create new compositions. Drawing from a range of ideas and piecing together already existing musical ideas, new innovations can be developed. Students create mash-ups by interviewing others and discovering how music can be connected with meaningful moments and relationships in one's life, which is the essence of personal narrative and memoir writing. Creating mash-ups also encourages students to bring the culture and history of their families into the classroom and share meaningful memories with others.

Soundscapes

In this strategy, students create a sense of setting through the layering of sound effects. Students "analyze a particular event or situation purely through sound and then recreate it. The audience listens to the performance with eyes closed while the performers, if successful, bring the environment immediately and accurately to life through sound alone. The audience will feel as if they are immersed in the soundscape, whether it be the rainforest, a desert oasis, a moment in the Civil War, Napoleon's March, or a moment in time from a chapter book the class is reading. The challenge for the performers is to carefully select just the essential sounds and place them sequentially in such a way that produces an accurate reproduction of the sound environment" (Donovan and Pascale 2012).

Found Sounds

Model Lesson: Onomatopoeia

Model Lesson Overview

Students explore *onomatopoeia*, or words that represent sounds, in a text. They examine how the author purposefully uses words that make sounds. In pairs, students collect found sounds around the classroom to enhance the scenes in a text. One partner plays the sound, and the other partner chooses a word to represent the sound. Partners play their musical found sounds as the story is read aloud to the class once again, creating and arranging a composition.

Standards

K–2

- Uses descriptive words to convey basic ideas

- Uses a variety of sound sources when composing

3–5

- Uses descriptive and precise language that clarifies and enhances ideas

- Performs simple pieces with appropriate dynamics

- Performs simple pieces in rhythm

6–8

- Uses descriptive language that clarifies and enhances ideas

- Uses a variety of nontraditional sound sources when composing and arranging

9–12

- Uses precise and descriptive language that clarifies and enhances ideas and supports different purposes

- Understands the traditional uses of various sound sources

Materials

- Various household items that produce sound (athletic shoes that squeak, utensils to rub together, etc.)

- Book that features onomatopoeia

- *Our Sound Words* (page 104, soundwords.pdf)

Found Sounds *(cont.)*

Preparation

Prior to the lesson, have students collect sounds for homework. Their job is to find objects that make interesting sounds and bring them to class the next day. Each student should bring in one or two items. Give them examples of items they could find, such as an athletic shoe that squeaks, kitchen utensils that could be struck and rubbed against each other, or tinfoil to be crunched. You should also gather a couple of items to add variety to the collection or to give to students who forget to bring one.

Select a book that features onomatopoeia, such as *Blackout* by John Rocco or *Planting the Wild Garden* by Kathryn Galbraith. Additional ideas are provided in the Specific Grade Level Ideas.

Procedure

1. Discuss the meaning of *found sounds* by having students share the sounds that they found. Provide time for students to experiment with the "instruments" in small groups and explore different ways they can be used to make sounds. Encourage students to find more than one way to make a sound with each item. For example, they can blow on the top of a bottle, shake it with pennies or pebbles inside, or roll it. Provide time for students to share their discoveries about new ways to make sounds.

2. Discuss the word *onomatopoeia* by talking about the use of sound words in stories. Share a book that features onomatopoeia with vivid suggestions of sound. As you read, point out the author's use of onomatopoeia with sound words. Have students close their eyes and create mental images as you read these words. Discuss with students how these sounds help to create meaning for the reader.

3. Record a class list of onomatopoeic words for students to reference throughout the lesson. Start with the words from the book you read. Then, add additional examples as a class. You may even decide to research *onomatopoeia* online. Some words that can be added include *crackle*, *hiss*, *splash*, *whoosh*, and *sizzle*.

4. Tell students that they will create found sounds to enhance their understanding of the story. Divide students into pairs, and assign each pair a scene or event from the story. Tell students that they will work with their partners to collect items to be used as found sounds.

5. Distribute *Our Sound Words* (page 104) to students. Tell students that one partner will make a sound and record it on the chart. The other partner will name the sound with an onomatopoeic word and record it on the chart. Then, partners will work together to write how their sound enhances the scene. Partners will continue this process to create three found sounds.

Found Sounds *(cont.)*

6. Reread the story to the class. Have partners play their found sounds when their section of the story is read. As they do, ask follow-up questions. Use the Questions for Discussion to guide discussion.

Questions for Discussion

- How did making new sounds help you to understand your section of the story?

- Which sounds do you prefer? Why?

- In what ways was reading the story together with the sounds like a musical composition in which sounds are played together?

- How do sounds impact your experience of the story?

- How and why might you use onomatopoeia in your own writing?

Specific Grade Level Suggestions

K–2

Complete *Our Sound Words* as a whole class. Then, as you reread the story, call on different students or pairs of students to demonstrate sounds for the rest of the class.

As an extension, take students outside to listen for sounds. The sound outing could be to the cafeteria or to the playground. Have students bring along their writer's notebooks and list words that come to mind upon hearing the sounds. Have students revisit their own writing pieces and find a meaningful place to add a word that represents a sound. Consider using *Planting the Wild Garden* by Kathryn Galbraith to further explore onomatopoeia.

3–5

Explore some of the found sounds brought in from home. Have the class listen with their eyes closed to keep the source of the sound a secret. After hearing the found sound, have students write in their writing notebooks to explore the following questions: What do the sounds remind you of? Who or what would make these sounds? What images come to mind upon hearing the sounds? The source of the found sound is then revealed. This notebook entry can serve as an idea for a future piece of writing.

Found Sounds *(cont.)*

6–8

Have students choose a setting, scene, or chapter from a myth, drama, poem, or any chapter book they are reading. Ask them to collect items to use as found sounds that will enhance the meaning of the words. Students can also create a composition using their found sounds. In order to create a composition, have students determine who will play which found sound and in what order. Will they play all at once or take turns? Will the found sounds overlap? Have students perform their structure while an excerpt from the myth, drama, poem, or chapter is read aloud. Ask students to choose words to represent their found sounds and create a poem that includes the words. Students can then revisit their own writing pieces and add meaningful onomatopoeia. Students can imagine that they are on a radio show and bringing their text to life through sound.

9–12

Have students collect found sounds from instruments, the Internet, and the environment and create new onomatopoeic words using these sounds. Create class lists of these new sound words, and have students draft stories or poetry using descriptive language and including these new found words. Have students create a composition of found sounds that tells a sound story. Then, add words to supplement the composition.

Name _____ Date _____

Our Sound Words

Directions: Think about the event in the book. Then, collect found sounds that enhance the meaning. Choose a word to represent your sound, or create a new word.

Found Sound	How did you create the sound?	What is the name of your found sound?	How does your found sound tell more about the event in the story?
#1			
#2			
#3			

Songwriting

Model Lesson: Understanding a Tall-Tale Character

Model Lesson Overview

Students demonstrate knowledge of tall tales by writing new lyrics to an original song. After reading a variety of tall tales, students listen to an original ballad about Johnny Appleseed. Students become familiar with the melody of the ballad. They write original lyrics to tell the story of a different tall-tale character, using the melody of the ballad. Depending on the grade level, students can write an original chorus and one verse or write an entire song.

Standards

K–2

- Knows the main characters in a story
- Sings invented songs

3–5

- Knows the defining characteristics and structural elements of a variety of literary genres
- Sings ostinatos, partner songs, and rounds

6–8

- Understands elements of character development
- Sings with good breath control, expression, and technical accuracy at a level that includes modest ranges and changes of tempo, key, and meter

Materials

- Audio recording: "The Ballad of Johnny Appleseed" (balladjohnnyappleseed.mp3)
- *The Ballad of Johnny Appleseed* (pages 108–109, ballad.pdf)
- *Lyric Brainstorming Guide* (page 110, lyricguide.pdf)
- *Songwriting Planner* (page 111, songwriting.pdf)
- Audio recording: "The Ballad of Johnny Appleseed" (instrumental version) (instrumentalappleseed.mp3)

Songwriting (cont.)

Preparation

This model lesson is a culminating activity, so make sure that students understand the characteristics of tall tales and have read different tall tales as a class. Decide how you wish to group students as they plan for their song adaptation. Locate "The Ballad of Johnny Appleseed" by David Williams on the Digital Resource CD (balladjohnnyappleseed.mp3). Make student copies of the lyrics or be ready to display them using available technology. See the Specific Grade Level Ideas for additional ideas.

Procedure

1. Review the characteristics of a tall tale with students. Discuss the ways in which exaggeration is part of all tale tales. Talk about examples of special abilities that characters in tall tales often possess and how those abilities become part of the story.

2. Distribute *The Ballad of Johnny Appleseed* (pages 108–109) to students. Then, play "The Ballad of Johnny Appleseed" (balladjohnnyappleseed.mp3). Have the class follow along with the lyrics.

3. Discuss how the song tells the story of a tall-tale character. Have students find evidence of the unique characteristics of tall tales and talk about those as a class.

4. Introduce the terms *melody, lyric, chorus,* and *verse.* Discuss how the chorus in the song about Johnny Appleseed reveals the main idea and the verses provide details. Give students multiple opportunities to sing along and become familiar with the melody of "The Ballad of Johnny Appleseed."

5. Tell students that they will be writing their own ballads based on a tall-tale character. Distribute *Lyric Brainstorming Guide* (page 110) to students. Ask students to choose a tall tale character and complete the *Lyric Brainstorming Guide* to develop a rhyming structure for their lyrics, brainstorming potential words that rhyme with the word ending each line.

6. Distribute *Songwriting Planner* (page 111) to students. Have students use the handout to write original lyrics for a chorus and one verse about the tall-tale character they chose, using the melody of "The Ballad of Johnny Appleseed."

7. Have students share their songs with partners or the class, singing their original lyrics along with the instrumental version of "The Ballad of Johnny Appleseed" (instrumentalappleseed.mp3).

8. Use the Questions for Discussion to talk with students about using the process of songwriting to better understand a tall-tale character.

Songwriting *(cont.)*

Questions for Discussion

- How did you decide what information to include in your lyrics?

- What were the challenges of songwriting?

- How did songwriting help you understand a character and/or the events of his or her life?

Specific Grade Level Ideas

K–2

As a class, brainstorm ideas to create lyrics and adapt a simple song that students know well. Work with students to learn the song and sing it together. Songs can be written about many different types of literature and genres. Short songs can be used that do not require multiple verses and a chorus.

3–5

Challenge students to write additional verses to tell details about their tall-tale characters. Have students explore how a song can communicate the humor of tall tales. Share humorous folk tale characters such as the characters in *Emily's Fortune* by Phyllis Reynolds Naylor.

6–8

Students can use a variety of folk legends as mentor texts as they write an original folk legend. They can also learn about the origin of ballads. Using a Venn diagram, have students compare and contrast folk legends with ballads. Have students write an original folk legend and turn it into an original ballad. Students can use the melody of "The Ballad of Johnny Appleseed" by David Williams or create their own melodies.

Name _____   Date _____

The Ballad of Johnny Appleseed

"The Ballad of Johnny Appleseed"
by David Williams

(Chorus)
Johnny, Johnny Appleseed
Friend of the pioneer, knew no greed
Planted trees, so all could feed
You could always count on Appleseed.

(Verse 1)
There was a man, once walked this land,
A bag of apple seeds in his hand,
3,000 miles, from sea to sea
Sowing apples and prosperity.
John Chapman was his rightful name
Long before he rose to fame.
At an early age he knew tragedy
When his mama died before he turned three.

(Repeat Chorus)

(Verse 2)
Young John found peace in the fields and woods
Learning everything that he could,
He befriended the otter, raccoon, and deer—
They sensed his goodness and felt no fear.
His love of nature grew and grew
Before too long, he knew what to do.
So he set forth from the family nest
To ease the burden of those out West.

(Repeat Chorus)

The Ballad of Johnny Appleseed *(cont.)*

(Verse 3)

He traveled far to Ohio,
A barefoot lad trudging through the snow,
He shrugged off rain, sleet, and fog
And he weathered storms in a hollow log.
Johnny made no enemies
A friend like this was a friend indeed!
Whether pioneer or native man
John shared his seeds and a helping hand.

(Repeat Chorus)

(Verse 4)

And soon his fame began to grow
Like the trees that grew from the seeds he'd sow.
Far and wide they'd tell the tale
Of the appleseed man on the westward trail.
John Chapman faded into history
As Johnny Appleseed came to be—
A hero, a myth, a sage, a seer,
A legend throughout the Wild Frontier.

(Repeat Chorus)

(Verse 5)

Now every apple must ripen and fall—
Johnny knew this best of all.
An old man now, he took to bed
And within three days, the great man was dead.
But the stories died not with old John
For a legend lives on proud and strong!
Long past the time when the real life ends
The stories are passed among kin and friends.

(Repeat Chorus × 2)

Printed with Permission: Title—"Early Tracks"—including several songs, one of which is "The Ballad of Johnny Appleseed" Author/Copyright Claimant/Rights and Permissions—David George Alexander Williams, Registration #:SRu 1-082-776, Date: July 27, 2012

Name _____ Date _____

Lyric Brainstorming Guide

Directions: Use the chart to help you plan your song lyrics.

Tall Tale Character:	
Character Traits/Description (exaggeration, special skills, etc.):	**Ballad Events:**
Lyric Ideas:	**Potential Rhymes:**

Name _____ Date _____

Songwriting Planner

Directions: Use the chart to help you plan your song structure.

Title of Song (tall-tale character)

```
┌ ─ ─ ─ ─ ─ ─ ─ ─ ─ ─ ─ ─ ─ ─ ─ ─ ─ ─ ─ ─ ─ ─ ┐
│                                              │
│                                              │
└ ─ ─ ─ ─ ─ ─ ─ ─ ─ ─ ─ ─ ─ ─ ─ ─ ─ ─ ─ ─ ─ ─ ┘
```

Chorus (important ideas about the character)

```
┌ ─ ─ ─ ─ ─ ─ ─ ─ ─ ─ ─ ─ ─ ─ ─ ─ ─ ─ ─ ─ ─ ─ ┐
│                                              │
│                                              │
│                                              │
│                                              │
│                                              │
│                                              │
└ ─ ─ ─ ─ ─ ─ ─ ─ ─ ─ ─ ─ ─ ─ ─ ─ ─ ─ ─ ─ ─ ─ ┘
```

Verse (details about the character)

```
┌ ─ ─ ─ ─ ─ ─ ─ ─ ─ ─ ─ ─ ─ ─ ─ ─ ─ ─ ─ ─ ─ ─ ┐
│                                              │
│                                              │
│                                              │
│                                              │
│                                              │
│                                              │
└ ─ ─ ─ ─ ─ ─ ─ ─ ─ ─ ─ ─ ─ ─ ─ ─ ─ ─ ─ ─ ─ ─ ┘
```

Chants

Model Lesson: Main Idea in Nonfiction Narratives

Model Lesson Overview

Students read a narrative informational text and explore the main idea by writing and performing chants with six to eight lines layered on top of each other. Through this process, students go back to the text and reread to find specific words and phrases that show the main idea and supporting details. They decide when to include specific words or phrases from the book in their chants and when to put ideas into their own words.

Standards

K–2	3–5
• Understands the main idea and supporting details of simple expository information • Sings invented songs	• Includes main idea when summarizing or paraphrasing a reading selection • Includes supporting details when summarizing or paraphrasing information • Improvises simple rhythmic and melodic embellishments on familiar melodies

6–8

• Summarizes and paraphrases information in texts

• Improvises melodic embellishments and simple rhythmic and melodic variations

Materials

• Narrative informational text

• *Sample Chants* (page 116, chants.pdf)

• *Planning for Chant* (page 117, planningchant.pdf)

Preparation

Locate a narrative nonfiction text such as *The Wolves Are Back* or *The Buffalo Are Back* by Jean Craighead George. Review *Sample Chants* (page 116) and *Planning for Chant* (page 117). Additional ideas are provided in the Specific Grade Level Ideas.

Chants *(cont.)*

Procedure

1. Share a narrative informational text with students. When you are finished reading the text, discuss the main idea. Model how to scan back through the text to find specific evidence for the main idea. Record students' ideas for them to reference throughout the lesson as they list words or phrases that describe the main idea. Discuss the supporting details and work together as a class to locate evidence in the text. Pull out these details and record them for students to reference.

2. Explain to students that one way to further explore the main idea and supporting details of a text is through chants. Explain that in a chant, each line is sung or spoken by a group in a particular rhythmic pattern and pitch (high or low vocal tone). Introduce the musical term ostinato as a repetition of similar rhythmic patterns and tones.

3. Introduce students to the idea of *rhythm* (repeating beat), *dynamics* (softness or loudness of the voice), and *pitch* (high or low sound of the vocal tone). Use the *Sample Chants* (page 116) to provide students with practice using these three components of chanting. Then, explain that the chants can be layered on top of each other. Different versions of the same lines can be spoken or sung simultaneously.

4. Tell students that they will be chanting the *Sample Chants* as a class. To facilitate the first chant, divide students into groups to practice layering the phrases of the chant. One group chants the repeated first line in a slow, low-pitched rhythm: "The wolves are back; the wolves are back." Then, as the first group continues repeating their lines, the next group of students layers "The valley is sharing food again!" with a medium pitch and rhythm. Then, the next group adds another layer to the chant with "The grasses are growing tall again!," similarly chanted with a medium pitch and rhythm. Continue adding layers until all lines are chanted. Discuss with students how the chant expresses the main idea of the text and how the chant shows the evolution of what happens over time—that when the wolves come back, the environmental balance is restored.

5. To facilitate the second chant, divide students into groups of six to chant the opening stanza. Have one group begin chanting, "The wolves are gone," and have additional groups add to the chant when their lines are to be read. Eventually, all lines will be read simultaneously, allowing for students to stop chanting line by line until "The wolves are gone" is the last line chanted. Repeat the process with the second stanza. Ask students to discuss the characteristics of the chant. Work as a group to identify the main idea and supporting details of the chant, discussing how the chant shows the relationship between a series of ideas linked to a dramatic moment and how each line adds new perspective to the idea.

Chants *(cont.)*

6. Tell students that they will work in small groups to create their own chants, summarizing the meaning of the narrative informational text. Remind students to use words or phrases that show the main idea of the text, and then add details to support the main idea. Refer students back to the list recorded earlier in the lesson. Tell students that they will need to decide when to use specific words and phrases from the book and when to paraphrase. Have students complete Planning for Chant (page 117) in small groups and create their chant. Use the Planning Questions to guide students' thinking.

7. Invite students to add instrumental sounds (these can be found items that make sounds or musical instruments if available) to go with each line and then do the chant with words only, words and instruments, and instruments only.

8. Have each group perform their chant for the class. Debrief using the Questions for Discussion.

Planning Questions

- What pitch will you use?

- What dynamics will you use?

- What rhythms are suggested by the words in your line?

- What other sound effects can you add to give your phrase more interest (the use of instruments, clapping, stomping, slapping the desk, and so forth)?

- Are there gestures you could add to emphasize your tempo or heighten the impact of a particular verse (slow, curved motions or quick, jagged movements)?

Questions for Discussion

- Which words or phrases show the main idea of the text?

- Which words or phrases show details that support the main idea?

- How did you decide when to paraphrase and when to quote from the text?

- How and why did you include figurative language?

- How did the rhythm of the lines work when the lines were overlapped?

- How did the different pitch, dynamic, and rhythm affect the way lines sound together?

- What other ideas could you experiment with to make your chant more interesting?

Chants *(cont.)*

Specific Grade Level Ideas

K–2

Have students create the chant as a class and then add an additional part on their own. Consider using the book *Rah, Rah, Radishes! A Vegetable Chant* by April Pulley Sayre as a mentor text. Students can also use chanting to internalize letter-sound relationships, word patterns, and the spelling of high-frequency words. Invite students to come up with ideas for a kinesthetic component to the chant, such as clapping, jumping in place, or tapping as they chant. Have students work on creating chants with interesting sounds and rhythms. Discuss the creative aspects of the chants as well as the sound relationships. Spend a few minutes chanting the spelling of commonly used words. Encourage students to create their own chants to remember spellings and patterns of words.

3–5

In addition to the K–2 Specific Grade Level Ideas, extend this lesson by dividing students into small groups to create a chant for another nonfiction text, such as *The Buffalo Are Back* by Jean Craighead George. Students can create chants to remember conventions of spelling, commonly misspelled words, vowel combinations, and contractions.

6–8

Ask students to select phrases that make the chants more complex with three overlapping lines. They will need to experiment with rhythm, dynamics, pitch, and word choice. The first line becomes the baseline of the chant, and the other lines layer on top. Students can also create chants to recall rules for irregular structural changes in spelling and for conventions of capitalization and punctuation.

Sample Chants

Sample Chant for *The Wolves Are Back* by Jean Craighead George

The wolves are back; the wolves are back
The valley is sharing food again!

The wolves are back; the wolves are back
The grasses are growing tall again!

The wolves are back; the wolves are back
Hikers marvel at the sound.

The wolves are back; the wolves are back
Trees grow, erosion stops.

The wolves are back; the wolves are back
Balance is restored!

Sample Chant for *The Wolves Are Back* by Jean Craighead George

The wolves are gone
Where did they go?
Gone…. Everyone
No voices howling
Chorus of the wilderness
Silenced

The wolves are back
Jogging through the grass
The valley is sharing food again
Hunting bison
Carcass of elk
H—O—W—L

Name _____ Date _____

Planning for Chant

Directions: Answer the questions to help plan for your chant.

What specific words in the text show the main idea?

_____

_____

Using just one sentence or phrase, summarize the main idea in your own words.

_____

_____

What supporting details will you include in your chant?

_____

_____

What line or lines will you repeat?

_____

_____

How can you work with different syllables to create interesting rhythms?

_____

_____

Is there figurative language that you can use? List some examples.

_____

_____

What information will you paraphrase, or put in your own words?

_____

_____

Mash-Up

Model Lesson: Meaningful Memories

Model Lesson Overview

In this lesson, students use music to represent stories and culture that are passed down from earlier generations. Students interview a family member or special person in their lives to learn about his or her favorite song from the past. They inquire about the memories attached to the song—memories of people, places, or experiences. Students write down the lyrics to the chorus of the song and bring the lyrics to class. They combine these lyrics with the chorus of their own favorite song to create a mash-up and write about the meaning.

Standards

K–2
- Asks and responds to questions
- Understands the relationship between music and history and culture

3–5
- Listens to classmates and adults
- Understands the relationship between music and history and culture

6–8
- Asks questions to seek elaboration and clarification of ideas
- Understands the relationship between music and history and culture

9–12
- Uses a variety of strategies to enhance listening comprehension
- Understands the relationship between music and history and culture

Materials

- Story about how families bond through music
- *Interview Planner* (pages 122–123, interviewplan.pdf)
- Scissors
- Glue

Preparation

Select a text with a theme of family connections and music such as the memoir *Grandma's Records* by Eric Velasquez.

Mash-Up *(cont.)*

Procedure

1. Begin with a discussion about personal connections that all of us have to certain music, asking such questions as, "Do you have a favorite song?" "Why is it special to you?" "How can a song remind us of a special person, place, or experience?" "What songs are special to your family members?" "How can you find out?"

2. Share a text about family bonding through music. One suggested title is *Grandma's Records* by Eric Velasquez, but you may choose an alternate text that is appropriate and interesting to your students.

3. Introduce the concept of a *mash-up* by explaining to students that it is a way in which musicians assemble parts from a variety of songs or music to create a new composition. Share the musical terms that you'll be referencing in this strategy, including *melody* (the tune of a song), *lyrics* (the words in a song), *chorus* (the repeating lines of a song), and *verse* (repeating melody with different lyrics).

4. Explain to students that they will be creating a mash-up of their own by using their favorite song as well as a family member's favorite song. Tell students that they will be exploring the idea of deepening family bonds through music by interviewing a family member or a special person about music. Distribute *Interview Planner* (pages 122–123) to students. Have students complete their interviews for homework and bring them back to class.

5. Ask students to choose a favorite song and write down the lyrics to the chorus. Then, explain to students that they will create a musical mash-up by combining the lyrics of their favorite songs with the lyrics of a family member's favorite songs in a creative way. Students should cut out lines from the written lyrics and glue them together in new ways. Use the Planning Questions to guide students' thinking.

6. Have students sing (to themselves, if desired) the musical mash-up in order to hear how the two melodies alternate and work together.

7. Invite students to share their mash-ups with others if they are comfortable doing so. Discuss the process with students, using the Questions for Discussion.

8. Encourage students to share the mash-up with the family member or special person they interviewed.

Mash-Up *(cont.)*

Planning Questions

- Which lines from your favorite song do you want to include?

- Which lines from your family member's song will you include?

- How are these lines important to you and your family?

- How well do these lines work together to create a new song?

- How will you put the pieces of the songs together so that transitions flow?

Questions for Discussion

- What did you learn about music and memories from your interview process?

- What types of things did people remember through song?

- What challenges are involved in creating a mash-up?

- How is your mash-up meaningful to you?

Specific Grade Level Ideas

K–2

Take a class poll by having students vote for their favorite song from a list of songs that they sing together in school—songs from the classroom or from music class. Share with students your own favorite song from your childhood. Using the chorus and lyrics from the two songs, work as a class to create a mash-up that combines the students' favorite song and your favorite song (or another student's). Use sentence strips to record lyrics, and then have students help you move lines around to create the perfect mash-up. Have students glue the mash-up lyrics into their writing notebooks and write or draw a picture to describe some part of the song that is memorable.

3–5

Have students glue a copy of their mash-up into their writer's notebooks and describe the memories attached to their favorite song by writing in their journals. This notebook entry can serve as an idea for future writing pieces. Use this process to begin a study of personal narrative writing and explore voice in writing.

Mash-Up *(cont.)*

6–8

Use this process to spark a discussion about memoir writing. Have memoirs available for students to read and examine. As a class, brainstorm the characteristics of memoir writing. Have students write a memoir that shows the special relationship between themselves and another person in their lives.

Invite students to work in pairs to create mash-ups of songs that both students enjoy. Make sure that students pay attention to how the language of the songs flows and how the meanings of the lyrics fit together in some way that makes sense musically.

9–12

Have students be responsible for selecting both songs to combine in a mash-up. This could be done in the context of many different language arts topics as a way to demonstrate character analysis, theme, tone, or author's purpose. Nonfiction texts could also work well with this activity, with a mash-up to represent the ideas behind a biography or to represent a persuasive argument.

Name _____   Date _____

Interview Planner

Directions: Interview a family member or special person in your life, using the following questions. Then, write and ask two of your own questions.

Person's name: _____

Relationship to me: _____

What is one of your favorite songs from the past?

_____

Why do you still remember this song?

_____

_____

What is most meaningful about the words of the song?

_____

_____

What is most meaningful about the tune?

_____

_____

In what ways is this song connected to your family traditions?

_____

_____

_____

Interview Planner *(cont.)*

Tell me about the special people, places, or experience that you think about when you hear the song.

_____

_____

_____

Write the lyrics to the chorus here:

_____

_____

_____

_____

_____

Write and ask two of your own questions:

1. _____

   _____

   _____

2. _____

   _____

   _____

Soundscapes

Model Lesson: Exploring Settings

Model Lesson Overview

In this strategy, students listen to a text that takes place in a richly detailed setting. Students work together to determine the characteristics of settings within a text. Then, they locate sensory descriptions in the text that bring the setting to life by layering sounds to represent one or more settings.

Standards

K–2

- Knows the setting in a story
- Uses a variety of sound sources when composing

3–5

- Understands differences in literary works in terms of setting
- Understands the use of imagery in literary texts
- Creates and arranges music to accompany readings or dramatizations

6–8

- Understands the effects of imagery on the reader
- Identifies and analyzes the elements of setting
- Knows how the elements of music are used to achieve unity and variety, tension and release, and balance in musical compositions

Materials

- Text with multiple evocative settings
- *The Sounds of a Setting* (page 128, sounds.pdf)

Preparation

Select a book to share with students that has multiple or evocative settings, such as *The Tin Forest* by Helen Ward or *Bringing the Rain to Kapiti Plain* by Verna Aardema. Decide if you will have students use found sounds or percussion instruments, such as triangles or drums, to create music. They can also vocalize and create sounds using their voices. If using instruments, gather those ahead of time. Additional ideas are provided in the Specific Grade Level Ideas.

Soundscapes (cont.)

Procedure

1. Share the story that you have chosen to read aloud. Read it aloud once for enjoyment. Ask students questions that focus on setting, such as, "What are some specific sensory images in the text that communicate the setting?" "In what ways does the change of setting move the story along?" Invite students to close their eyes (if they are comfortable) and pay attention to sensory details they imagine as the story is read.

2. Review the story with the class and ask students to help you locate specific sensory images that describe the setting. Review with students how sensory images help readers see, hear, feel, touch, smell, and taste images that are described in a text. Discuss the qualities of each unique setting.

3. Introduce the concept of a *soundscape*. Explain to students that a soundscape is a layering of sound effects that will help them recreate a place or event. It is a way for students to bring a story to life by using sound alone. Tell students that they will recreate and give life to a particular setting from the story they have heard or read.

4. Divide students into groups according to the settings in the book. Have groups complete *The Sounds of a Setting* (page 128). Explain to students that this chart will help them plan their soundscapes. Students will work together in groups to identify the ways that the setting is described using sensory images, as well as the sounds that can be used to recreate this place.

5. Have groups use percussion instruments, found sounds, and/or their voices and practice playing sounds together that reflect the setting. Use the Planning Questions to stimulate students' thinking. Provide adequate time for groups to rehearse their soundscapes.

6. Have groups share their soundscapes with the class. Then, tell students that all groups will come together to form one ensemble. Explain that you will read the story, and as each setting unfolds, the group assigned to that setting will perform their soundscape as a backdrop to the text.

7. Read the story aloud as the soundscapes are shared. Using the Questions for Discussion, explore how the sense of setting deepens the message of the book and how music helped students understand the settings. Invite students to write additional sensory images to describe the setting.

Soundscapes (cont.)

Planning Questions

- How might you bring this sensory aspect of a scene to life through a soundscape?

- As you listen to the story, what sounds and images do you imagine?

- What other sound ideas could fit within the setting?

- How do you connect to each setting? What does it make you remember or feel in your own life?

- How might a soundscape enhance the reading of a text?

Questions for Discussion

- In what ways did the soundscapes help you understand each setting in the story?

- In what ways did the soundscapes help you understand how the settings changed?

- What sensory images from the book helped you create the soundscape?

- How did the creation of a soundscape bring each distinct setting to life?

- As you tried different choices in your soundscape, what results did you get with creating a composition that captured the setting?

- What struck you about the soundscape presentations of other groups?

Specific Grade Level Ideas

K–2

As a class, complete *The Sounds of a Setting* or divide the class in half and focus on only two significant settings. Invite students to write about their favorite sounds and why those sounds best match the settings they represent.

Students can also work in larger groups to represent other aspects of a story, using sounds such as important events, character mood or emotion, or suspenseful and climactic scenes. Ask students to consider the feelings or thoughts that are evoked during these parts of the story.

Soundscapes *(cont.)*

3–5

Extend this lesson by inviting students to locate sensory images that describe the setting in the books they are reading. Small groups can create an ensemble with a conductor to explore how the settings are similar and different. *The Tin Forest* by Helen Ward allows for a careful examination of how writers hook their readers by creating a lead about the setting. In addition to the setting lead, writers also show (not tell) through alliteration, strong verbs, sensory images, repeated lines, personification, and snapshots in their books.

6–8

Small groups can create an ensemble with a conductor and experiment with conducting cues such as tempo (speed) and dynamics (volume) in relation to the setting, characters, and progression of story events. Students can explore the differences among settings of different genres. Students can view an orchestra and conductor in progress and create a story with settings inspired by the music.

Name _____ Date _____

The Sounds of a Setting

Directions: Use the chart to take notes from the book that will help you plan your soundscape.

Setting	
Sensory images in the story (What do you see, hear, feel, taste, and smell?)	
Creating a soundscape (What sounds can be put together to create a sense of setting?)	
Ideas for creating the soundscape, using or creating instruments and found sounds	
Notes on where to insert sounds to match the text	

Poetry

#51090—*Strategies to Integrate the Arts in Language Arts*

Poetry

Understanding Poetry

Poetry engages students in writing, reading, speaking, and listening. Creating poems can capture the essence of an idea. As stated by Polly Collins, "When students create poems about topics of study, they enhance their comprehension through the connections they have made between the topic and their own lives, the topic and the world around them, and the poetry and the content texts they have read" (2008, 83). Developing understanding of language arts through the creation of poems allows students to consider concepts related to language arts in new ways and to share their understanding through language and metaphor. Often, students enjoy creating poems but are not sure how to begin. The strategies provide guidance that will help students identify and work with rich language to explore the intricacies of language arts. Though poems often rhyme, they do not need to, and sentences don't need to always be complete. "We are more interested in 'surprising images' or words that have a special sound pattern. They empower students to be 'word-gatherers'" (McKim and Steinbergh 1992). Students are invited to put words together in unconventional ways, drawing on evocative language, playful juxtaposition of ideas, and creating images through words as they write poems about concepts in language arts. This active engagement changes students' relationships with language arts as they find their own language to describe what they know.

By working with poetic language, symbolism, and metaphors, students can deepen their understanding of ideas and develop their abilities to express. Dr. Janette Hughes (2007) notes that "poetry encourages an economy and precision in language that transfers to other types of oral and written communication."

Using poetry to explore language arts builds conceptual understanding. When your students become poets, they fine-tune their writing and explore the use of patterns, rhythm, and metaphor. Writing poems allows students to use language in fresh ways and develop a deeper understanding of language arts. As LaBonty and Danielson (2004) note, "it is obvious that both poetry and math rely on patterns and are dependent on students' skill with language, whether it is the language of verse and rhythm or the language of symbols and signs."

Poetry *(cont.)*

Strategies for Poetry

Dialogue Poem

Compare and contrast is one of the most effective instructional strategies that teachers can use (Marzano 2007). A dialogue poem encourages students to explore two different perspectives on a topic. This form of poetry works well with opposite but related concepts or perspectives. Similarities and differences between concepts can be explored, providing the rhythm and the feel of a dialogue. The poem is constructed by two writers, encouraging conversation about the content being explored and the ways to best translate ideas into poetic form. This collaborative work allows students to share what they know with their peers and to deepen learning. These poems also prompt students to better differentiate between two concepts being learned at the same time.

Rhyme and Rhythm

This strategy invites students to work in verse as ideas are translated into rhyming words and phrases. LaBonty notes that "a preference for rhyme and rhythm is contained in the linguistic make-up of all humans; rhyme is easier to recall than prose; rhythm helps carry the predictability of language. There is pattern and measure in every language and in the way we structure our lives" (1997). Though poems do not need to rhyme, rhymes can unify a poem, and the repeated sound can help to connect a concept in one line to that in another. Also, simple rhymes can serve as a memory device (Jensen 2008). Students are even more likely to remember poems they create themselves. Here, students are invited to explore their interpretations of poetry, the rhythmic patterns of poetry, and the various poetic devices as they read poetry aloud.

🔖 Juxtaposition

This strategy prompts students to find and collect words from a variety of sources and encourages placement of words and phrases in a variety of ways to reveal fresh language and insights. McKim and Steinbergh note that with word bowl poetry, "the very fact of manipulating the words, discarding some, trading others, adding what one needs for sense, can teach us something about selection and choice in making poems. Joining two or three words that normally don't appear together can make fresh images, charging them with new energy and excitement" (1992).

This strategy allows students to work with descriptions of concepts to create poems that reveal relationships and ideas about content in unique and enlightening language. Putting words together through juxtaposition allows students to boil ideas down to their essence. Students will benefit from having a range of words available from which to draw.

🔖 Bio Poems

This biographical strategy allows students to investigate traditions, attitudes, environmental influences, and commonly held perceptions about a particular idea or within a particular era. Inspired by George Ella Lyon (2010), bio poems follow a pattern using the phrase *I am from* and can be created through student responses to prompts (Kuta 2003). Using the senses to reflect on what has been seen, heard, smelled, touched, and tasted, students become aware of how they (or characters, fictional or real) have been shaped by their unique experiences. The observations and reflections help students become aware of how time and place can influence one's perspectives. When written about characters, students consider how context and background influence the development of a character's frame of reference.

🔖 Reversos

An inventive form of poetry has been introduced by Marilyn Singer (2010). Poems are written so that they are readable forward and backward. Both directions have a different meaning. These poems draw students' attention to how lines are linked, how meaning builds in different ways, and how phrasing can be turned on its head as lines are developed to work in both directions. In order to write this "two-poems-in-one," Singer gives this advice: "Writing a reverso is like playing a game. First, you need to let your mind relax. If you're writing about fairy tales, you need to find strong stories with dual points of view. If you're writing about other topics, you could start with a few lines that can be flipped—kind of like finding an image that's the core of the poem. You can build the poem from there. I use a lot of participles, infinitives, and single word sentences as well as things that can be turned into questions and interjections."

Dialogue Poems

Model Lesson: Compare and Contrast

Model Lesson Overview

Students read poems written for two voices and then work in groups to create their own dialogue poems. As they do so, they gain a deeper understanding of point of view and generate interest in the interweaving of voices around a common theme. These poems also prompt students to better differentiate between two opposite but related perspectives on the same event, a skill that is often required in reading both fiction and nonfiction texts.

Standards

K-2

- Describes the connection between two individuals, events, ideas, or pieces of information in a text

- Reads a variety of familiar literary passages and texts (e.g., poems)

3-5

- Uses point of view to write for a variety of purposes

- Knows the defining characteristics and structural elements of a variety of literary genres (e.g., poems)

6-8

- Establishes a point of view in narrative writing

- Knows the defining features and structural elements of a variety of literary genres (e.g., poems)

9-12

- Uses the writing technique of multiple viewpoints

- Knows the defining characteristics of a variety of literary forms and genres (e.g., poems)

Materials

- *Examples of Dialogue Poems* (pages 138–139, exampledialogue.pdf)

- *Two Voices Poem Plan* (page 140, twovoices.pdf)

Preparation

Familiarize yourself with the two examples of dialogue poems provided in *Examples of Dialogue Poems* (pages 138–139), or try writing one of your own. Note that each "side" of the poem is to be read by a different voice, and the lines in the middle by both voices. Additional ideas are provided in the Specific Grade Level Ideas.

Dialogue Poems *(cont.)*

Procedure

1. Display one or both of the dialogue poems in *Examples of Dialogue Poems* (pages 138–139) or share your own creation. Have two students read the different parts of the poem aloud.

2. Ask students, "What do you notice about how these poems are formed? What do you learn about each perspective? How do the poems reveal contrasting ideas? What do you notice about the lines read by both voices together? How does linking two voices in this poetic form generate interest for the reader?"

3. Invite students to remember and share a time they interacted with a person or animal. Tell students that the author of the poem "Chickadee," Amy Ludwig VanDerwater, wrote about an event from two points of view. She imagined something that she had really experienced and knew well: feeding chickadees out of her hand. She remembered her point of view: the feeling of holding a chickadee for a brief moment, and how it felt, tickly and lovely. She then thought about the chickadee's point of view and how huge and scary she must have appeared to the chickadee.

4. Have students think about a time when they interacted with an animal or pet. Have students consider what they were feeling, hoping, and wondering during this time. Then, have students think about what the animal would be feeling. Use the Planning Questions to guide discussion.

5. Offer the *Two Voices Poem Plan* (page 140) to students and provide them time to plan and create their dialogue poems.

6. Divide students into pairs. Each student will help the other perform his or her poem as dialogue poems are to be read by two voices. Provide students time to practice performing their poems aloud in two voices.

7. Have each pair present their dialogue poems to the rest of the class. Use the Questions for Discussion to guide discussion. If desired, students can record their performances and listen and discuss afterwards. You can also share these poems on a class blog or by using a tool that supports voice recording.

Dialogue Poems (cont.)

Planning Questions

- What feelings are associated with either point of view?

- What words or phrases are associated with each idea?

- How might you reveal the differences and similarities of either point of view?

- What shared ideas or central lines could you write that the voices could read together?

Questions for Discussion

- What differences did you identify between the points of view?

- What did you learn by writing your poems?

- What did you learn by listening to poems being read in two voices?

- What could you add to a poem you heard?

- What feedback could you give the authors?

- How did the poetic form bring ideas to life?

Specific Grade Level Ideas

K–2

Have students visit "The Poem Farm" at http://www.poemfarm.amylv.com to explore additional dialogue poems. Possible other topics include two different characters' perspectives in a story, ways to retell a story that differ according to perspective, or interpreting real-world events from different points of view.

Dialogue Poems *(cont.)*

3–5

Have students visit "The Poem Farm" at http://www.poemfarm.amylv.com to explore additional dialogue poems. Students can work with a partner on a dialogue poem after a group brainstorming session. In addition to the K–2 Specific Grade Level Ideas, students can learn about additional structures of dialogue poems, such as those in which the two voices share a line in order to show what they have in common. Share examples from *Joyful Noise: Poems for Two Voices* by Paul Fleischman.

Share informational texts with the compare-and-contrast structure, such as *Is My Dog a Wolf? How Your Dog Compares to Its Wild Cousin* by Jenni Bidner. Have students demonstrate their understanding of the similarities and differences between dogs and wolves by writing a dialogue poem.

With students, brainstorm a list of topics that you are exploring in the classroom. Invite students to create poems for two voices in order to compare and contrast opposite but related concepts. Topics may include two or more planets in the solar system or two types of insects from an informational text. You can also read "Fireflies" by Paul Fleischman, which is included in *Joyful Noise: Poems for Two Voices*, and compare the points of view of the fireflies and the main character who catches them.

6–8

Have students visit "The Poem Farm" at http://www.poemfarm.amylv.com to explore additional dialogue poems. Have pairs of students find two opposite perspectives from a newspaper article. Have them each take on one of the perspectives and have them go back and forth, creating a dialogue poem in the moment as they respond to the line written by the other. After writing as many lines as they can in the exploration of the issue, have them edit the dialogue to a short synopsis that captures the essence of the issue and the different vantage points.

9–12

Have students visit "The Poem Farm" at http://www.poemfarm.amylv.com to explore additional dialogue poems. Students can create poems around more advanced topics, such as the ways in which historical events are reported and discussed according to varying points of view or how an author's point of view can shape the way that information is shared in a nonfiction text.

Examples of Dialogue Poems

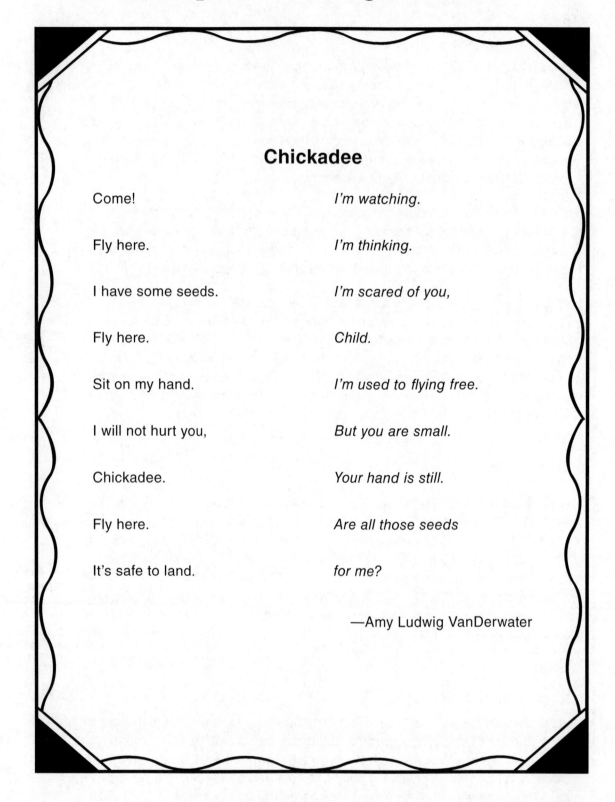

Chickadee

Come!	*I'm watching.*
Fly here.	*I'm thinking.*
I have some seeds.	*I'm scared of you,*
Fly here.	*Child.*
Sit on my hand.	*I'm used to flying free.*
I will not hurt you,	*But you are small.*
Chickadee.	*Your hand is still.*
Fly here.	*Are all those seeds*
It's safe to land.	*for me?*

—Amy Ludwig VanDerwater

Examples of Dialogue Poems (cont.)

Little Squirrel: A Poem in Two Voices

(Voice 1)

Little squirrel, you fell out of your tree!

Are you hurt? Don't worry.

You are safe with me.

(Voice 2)

Where am I? It's cold out here.

I want my warm nest

And my brothers near.

(Together)

Last night's strong winds still blow and blow.

(Voice 1)

Little squirrel, so frail and small,

I'll take you home

Before darkness falls.

(Voice 2)

Whose hand is this, so like my nest?

It's safe and warm,

I'll stay and rest.

(Together)

Sunset fades, a distant glow. Blue shadows lengthen upon deep snow.

(Voice 1)

Little squirrel, come with me.

And when you are grown,

I will set you free.

(Together)

Bright stars are out. Full moon hangs low,

As through the darkening woods we go...

—Brittany Williams

Dialogue Poems

Name _____ Date _____

Two Voices Poem Plan

Directions: You may find it helpful to brainstorm ideas for your dialogue poem before you begin writing. Use this form to play around with some ideas. Then, draft your poem in your writer's notebook or on a separate sheet of paper.

Summary of Event: _____

Poem Title: _____

Voice 1: _____

Thoughts and Ideas

_____

_____

_____

_____

_____

_____

Voice 2: _____

Thoughts and Ideas

_____

_____

_____

_____

_____

_____

_____

Rhyme and Rhythm

Model Lesson: Writing and Performing Poetry

Model Lesson Overview

Students explore the rhyme and rhythm of different poems by reading them aloud with expression. They investigate syllables and patterns by reading out loud while experimenting with volume, pace, rhythm, intonation, and pronunciation as they bring ideas in the poem to life. Students also share their thoughts about rhyming poems and nonrhyming poems. Finally, students practice performing their favorite poems to familiarize themselves with the rhyme and rhythm.

Standards

K–2

- Recites and responds to familiar stories, poems, and rhymes with patterns

- Reads aloud familiar stories, poems, and passages with fluency and expression

3–5

- Adjusts speed of reading to suit purpose and difficulty of the material

- Understands the ways in which language is used in literary texts (e.g., rhythm)

6–8

- Reads poetry appropriate to grades 6–8

- Understands the use of language in literary works to convey mood, images, and meaning (e.g., rhyme, voice, tone, sound)

Materials

- Variety of rhyming and nonrhyming poems and poetry books

- *Marking the Meaning* (page 145, meaning.pdf)

- *Tips for Performing Poetry* (page 144, tipspoetry.pdf)

Preparation

Gather a variety of rhyming and nonrhyming poems and review them. Select various poetry books for students to read so that they can browse through them and each choose a poem of interest. Additional ideas are provided in the Specific Grade Level Ideas.

Rhyme and Rhythm *(cont.)*

Procedure

1. Read a rhyming poem aloud, such as "The Road Not Taken" by Robert Frost. Choose a poem that is interesting and appropriate for the students in your class.

2. Read a nonrhyming poem aloud. Discuss the use of syllables and ask, "What do you like about nonrhyming poems?" Then, pair students and have each pair spend time reading through poems from a collection of poetry books. Ask students to find both rhyming and nonrhyming poems and think about pacing, patterns, and syllables as they read. Have students count out/clap out the rhythms. Ask, "What feels regular? Does the number of syllables in each line make a pattern? Does the pattern change? What do you like about poems that rhyme?"

3. Explain to students that they are going to practice reading poetry aloud. Distribute *Marking the Meaning* (page 145) to students. Tell students that they will each select a poem they would like to perform from the collection of poetry books and complete *Marking the Meaning*, looking for patterns and interesting moments in the poem.

4. Distribute the *Tips for Performing Poetry* (page 144) and discuss the suggested tips for performing poetry. Have students practice reciting their chosen poems and ask them to consider the tips. Ask students to think about the meaning of their poems and how they wish to express the meaning as they share their poems aloud.

5. Provide opportunities for the class to read and perform the poems several times. You could recite poems together as a class when walking to recess, gathering for meeting time, lining up at the door, or transitioning between lessons. Opportunities should feel natural. If desired, provide technology with voice-recording capabilities to aid with practice so that students can hear themselves reading the poem aloud.

6. Break students into small groups and have them rehearse their poems.

7. Have students perform their poems for the class. Compare and contrast rhyming and nonrhyming poems and the choices made when writing these poems. Use the Questions for Discussion to debrief students.

Rhyme and Rhythm *(cont.)*

Questions for Discussion

- What patterns did you find in different poems?
- What elements created the patterns (syllables, alliteration, onomatopoeia, etc.)?
- What sensory details did the poems bring to life?
- What metaphors and/or similes were effective?
- What do you enjoy about poems that rhyme?
- What do you enjoy about poems that do not rhyme?
- Why do some poets insist that poems are meant to be heard?

Specific Grade Level Ideas

K–2

Have students practice performing nursery rhymes, and as a class, write and perform their own nursery rhyme based on a theme of interest. Students can write rebus poems where they substitute images for words. You can also work with students to create nonrhyming acrostic poems where each letter of a word is the beginning letter for a word or phrase.

3–5

In addition to the K–2 Specific Grade Level Ideas, have students write their own poems using the process of writing and reading aloud to help edit poems based on hearing the development of specific patterns.

6–8

Have students choose a favorite song and treat the lyrics as a poem. Challenge them to play with the rhythm and rhyme until they're unrecognizable as the original song. Students can also examine the poetry of music by selecting their favorite lyrics, reciting them as a poem, and listening to them as they are performed in song. They can compare the feelings and emotions communicated through each format. Have students read, write, and perform poems as part of a poetry slam in which students read and recite their original work. Have students study a poem collection such as *Reflections on a Gift of Watermelon Pickle* compiled by Stephen Dunning, Edward Lueders, and Hugh Smith. Read students a "poem of the day" and have them reflect on the poetry in journals. Have students write poems that resonate with them personally.

Name _____ Date _____

Tips for Performing Poetry

Directions: Consider these helpful tips as you play around with different ways to recite a poem.

Tips to Consider
Think about how you want your audience to feel as you recite your poem.
Find parts that might be spoken loudly, quietly, quickly, or slowly.
Find a place in which you can pause for added effect.
Use facial expressions to match meaning.
Match the tone of your voice to the meaning of the lines.
Find a moment when you should look into the eyes of your audience members for added effect.

Name _____   Date _____

Marking the Meaning

Directions: Choose a poem and complete the chart.

Title of Poem and Author:	
What patterns do you notice in the poem?	
Does the poem rhyme? If so, what are the rhyming words?	
What catches your attention or surprises you in the poem?	
What is the poem about? What specific choices will you make in your performance to share the poem's meaning?	
What phrases are most striking?	

Juxtaposition

Model Lesson: Word Bowls and Found Poems

Overview

Students create poems using existing words and phrases they find in texts such as recipes, magazines, newspapers, song lyrics, clothing catalogs, letters, or their writer's notebooks. They choose words or phrases that speak to them—words that create mental images or spark interest. Students experiment with line breaks to create meaning and explore how the poem looks and sounds. Students are also encouraged to experiment with a variety of ways to juxtapose the words and may add others as needed.

Standards

K–2

- Writes in a variety of forms or genres
- Uses descriptive words to convey basic ideas

3–5

- Writes narrative accounts, such as poems and stories
- Uses descriptive and precise language that clarifies and enhances ideas

6–8

- Uses a variety of prewriting strategies
- Uses descriptive language that clarifies and enhances ideas

Materials

- Print materials with words that students can cut out (newspapers, catalogs, magazines, school flyers, menus, etc.)
- *Found Poem Example* (page 149, foundexample.pdf)
- Scissors
- Bowls or reusable containers

Preparation

Gather print materials so that students can choose words to be placed in word bowls and used in their found poetry. Familiarize yourself with the notion of found poetry. Additional ideas are provided in the Specific Grade Level Ideas.

Juxtaposition *(cont.)*

Procedure

1. Begin by activating students' prior knowledge about poetry by asking questions such as, "What poems have you read or written yourself? What makes a poem different from a story?" "Do poems have to rhyme?" "How are words, phrases, and sentences formatted in a poem?" "How do readers know when to pause while reading a poem aloud?" "Why would a poet include line breaks in a poem?"

2. Discuss how poets use different strategies when writing poetry. For example, some poets may have a plan in mind, such as looking for words about a specific topic. Other poets may choose random words that sound interesting and combine them in surprising ways to discover meaning.

3. Read aloud the *Found Poem Example* (page 149) to students. Explain that this poem was created by pulling words from a magazine article about Iceland in *National Geographic*. Explain how the words from the article were arranged in a special way to make meaning. Have students share their thoughts about the poem and the meaning that they understand from reading it.

4. Model for students how to browse through materials and use scissors to cut out significant words. Place those words in a bowl or other container. Ask students to help you draw several words from the bowl and create a class found poem by arranging the selected words. The idea is to put the words together in a variety of ways until they create a clear sense of the idea being explored. As appropriate, encourage metaphors, similes, and the use of imagery, sensory descriptors, and feeling words.

5. After you have completed an example together, students are ready to prepare for their own poems. Provide students with print materials and scissors. Each student should get a bowl or some kind of reusable container.

6. Have students individually create found poems by cutting words or phrases from magazines or other materials.

7. Tell students to rearrange the words they have found to create different line breaks and read each configuration aloud to hear the impact on meaning and rhythm. Have students also listen to other students read their poems aloud to determine if the poems sound the way they intend.

8. Ask students to choose their favorite configuration and read their poem aloud to the class. Discuss the process, using the Questions for Discussion.

Juxtaposition *(cont.)*

Questions for Discussion

- What did you learn through the process of creating your own poem?

- What unique or fresh language came out of the exploration of juxtaposing different words and phrases?

- What did you learn from listening to the poems of others?

Specific Grade Level Ideas

K–2

Students should work in small groups or as a class to create the found poem. Choose appropriate words from texts to explore for the word bowl activity. Discuss the use of punctuation and how readers know when to pause in the poem.

3–5

The activity can be used as written. Students can also read an article from a magazine, such as *TIME® for Kids*, *Ranger Rick*, or *National Geographic Kids™*. They can choose words and phrases that summarize the main idea of the article and present the main idea through a found poem. Students can also search for words to create figurative language such as metaphor, simile, and onomatopoeia.

6–8

Students can provide copies of their first drafts as well as their final poems along with individual reflections on the process. Have students choose passages from lengthy texts and convey the essence of meaning through a found poem. For example, how might a found poem capture the essence of a president's address to the nation?

Students can also use their writer's notebooks to record words they find online, such as blogs, and movies with subtitles. They can record the words on index cards, create a found poem, and rearrange the line breaks by moving the cards.

Found Poem Example

Iceland

by Sean Williams

3 million years ago, ice age

Ancient lava flows from a volcanic crater

Waterfall roars for centuries

Mossy islands, hot springs

Seabirds breed here, on an arch 40 feet high

Winter, at the far bank of the river

On an overlook after midnight, an outlaw

Is protected from the north wind

Bio Poems

Model Lesson: Character Context

Model Lesson Overview

This particular approach to a bio poem is called an "I Am From" poem. Students write an "I Am From" poem from the point of view of a character (real or imagined) in stories, magazine articles, nonfiction literature, newspapers, movies, plays, etc. "I Am From" poems were developed by teacher and writer George Ella Lyon (2010). She suggests a simple writing prompt for exploring personal histories and influences. Students begin each line with the phrase *I am from* and then introduce specific details of the character's lives such as special people, places, objects, influences, cultural traditions, foods, and sayings. This reflective process provides students with the opportunity to explore a character's frame of reference.

Standards

K–2

- Uses prewriting strategies to plan written work

- Uses descriptive words to convey basic ideas

3–5

- Uses strategies to draft and revise written work

- Uses descriptive and precise language that clarifies and enhances ideas

6–8

- Uses a variety of strategies to draft and revise written work

- Uses descriptive and precise language that clarifies and enhances ideas

9–12

- Uses a variety of prewriting strategies

- Uses precise and descriptive language that clarifies and enhances ideas and supports different purposes

Materials

- *I Am From Example 1* (page 154, iamfromexample1.pdf)

- *I Am From Example 2* (page 155, iamfromexample2.pdf)

- *I Am From Planner* (page 156, iamfromplanner.pdf)

Bio Poems *(cont.)*

Preparation

Read *I Am From Example 1* (page 154) or *I Am From Example 2* (page 155) to become familiar with how the format can be used to write about a literary character. You may wish to write an "I Am From" poem yourself to share with students. Additional ideas are provided in the Specific Grade Level Ideas.

Procedure

1. Introduce the notion of being "from" someplace. Have students tell how they would respond to someone who asks casually, "Where are you from?" Then, have them discuss what would be different if a good friend asked, "So how did you get to be you? What are things in your life that shaped or influenced you?"

2. Explain to students that they are going to choose a character in literature and write about his or her life story through poetry. Read the example provided in *I Am From Example 1* (page 154) or *I Am From Example 2* (page 155), depending on the level of your students, and have them discuss the ways in which the writers describe the character's experiences from the character's point of view.

3. Distribute the *I Am From Planner* (page 156) to students and have them discuss the various categories and possible responses. Consider adding additional prompts based on specific characters you are studying. You may wish to review the poem(s) you read in relation to the *I Am From Planner*. Use the Planning Questions to facilitate discussion.

4. After this overview, allow time for students to reflect and record words, phrases, or sentences about their literary characters.

5. Have students use their brainstormed words and phrases to create their own "I Am From" poems. Make sure students understand that they don't have to include all of the topics or all of the words they brainstormed within a topic.

6. Provide time for students to edit or confer about their poems in pairs. If this takes place on the following day, encourage students to talk with others who know the character through text, movies, or plays.

7. Have students practice presenting their poems orally, providing opportunities to rehearse reading a few times alone or with a peer.

8. Have students share and discuss their poems. Use the Questions for Discussion to lead discussion about the poems.

Bio Poems (cont.)

Planning Questions

- Who are the people who influenced your literary character? Why? How?

- What are the places or settings that influenced your character? Why? How?

- What are the objects that influenced your character? Why? How?

- What cultural traditions might the character have grown up with?

- What sayings might the character have heard or said?

- What interests or passions does the character have?

- What poetic devices can you use (e.g., repetition, metaphor, alliteration)?

Questions for Discussion

- What did you learn about the character?

- What are some ways our poems are different? The same?

- What are some examples of words or phrases that reveal where the character is from (places, experiences, people, objects)?

- As you heard the poems presented, what struck you about the characters' backgrounds and influences?

Specific Grade Level Ideas

K–2

Students should work together to create an "I Am From" poem as a class, selecting words and phrases to add as the teacher facilitates. As students write their own poems, you may have some students work with an adult who can record their thinking or use technology to record students' thoughts. Also consider the use of image with text (a rebus poem) to facilitate the process.

3–5

Students can interview each other in character using the graphic organizer. Have students write poems for a variety of characters in a text and have them introduce themselves in character as they read their poem.

Bio Poems *(cont.)*

6–8

Have students reflect specifically around a turning point or choice in a story and write the poem as a way to consider the character's stance on a particular issue. Have students build on the *I am from* stems by adding details and additional related lines.

9–12

In addition to the 6–8 Specific Grade Level Ideas, students can write a bio poem from the perspective of a larger concept, such as a career, an event, or a trend (e.g., "I am an architect…," "I am from the Industrial Revolution…").

I Am From Example 1

I Am From the Underground Railroad

Grades K–2

I am from the Underground Railroad
Traveling north
Guided by stars
And people who care
A few can make all the difference
Helping each other find freedom

Grades 3–5

I am from the South
Born into slavery
But freedom calls to me
And my family

I am from courage
Taking the risk to travel
Through the woods
Late at night
Little to eat and always scared
Trusting my instincts
Missing my family

I am from anticipation
Night after night
Northward bound
Follow the drinking gourd
My guiding path of stars

I Am From Example 2

I Am From Freedom

Grades 6–12

I am from the tidewater
eastern shore of Maryland
life in plantation slave quarters
yearning for freedom.

I am from "slow of speech, but quick to
    laugh,"
an "unteachable child"
sold....then returned to my owner when
    "I didn't work out."

I am from beatings
Crisscrossed scars across my back
Hiding—driven back by hunger
until I was older.

I am from the traplines
freeing muskrats from bondage
preparing me for bigger escapes.

I am from fieldwork
strong arms and back
Hearing tales of a pathway north.

I am from my father's training
stealth in the woods
creep without making a sound
barely breathing.

I am from escape
Making my fate alone
without my brothers.

I am from numerous points along a
    dangerous route
from bondage to freedom.

I am from the Underground Railroad
never seen but often spoke of
I am from duty—scout, spy, and nurse
depending on the need of the moment.

I am from Colonel Montgomery
and his regiment of one time slaves
rescuing eight hundred from slavery
in one daring night
scarcely breathing
heart pounding.

I am from icy rivers, and hiding in woods,
    wagons, and brush.

I am from courage
from speaking out and taking a stand.

I am from singing spirituals,
strains of "Go Down, Moses" wafting in
announcing my arrival
Come with me
I'll take you to the promised land.
Two trips a year
down to slave territory.

I am conductor on the Underground
    Railroad
Keep those wheels a movin' singing
Go Down, Moses...Go Down....

Inspired by Petry, Ann. 1955. *Harriet Tubman: Conductor
on the Underground Railroad*. New York: Harper Trophy.

Name _____ Date _____

I Am From Planner

Directions: Fill in the boxes to brainstorm ideas for an "I Am From" poem about a literary character. Then, on a separate sheet of paper, write your poem, beginning a line with "I am from" and developing the idea over one or more lines. Then, start fresh with "I am from" and add more ideas.

People the Character Knows:	**Places the Character Goes:**
Experiences the Character Has:	**Objects the Character Uses/Enjoys:**
The Character's Sayings:	**Traditions of the Character:**

Reversos

Model Lesson: Two Sides to Every Story

Model Lesson Overview

Students are introduced to the concept of *reverso* poems, which are poems that can be read forward and backward for a different meaning. Students learn how to read and comprehend reversos, modeling their poems from the teacher or Marilyn Singer's *Mirror Mirror: A Book of Reversible Verse*. They study how the use of punctuation, capitalization, and line breaks make a difference in meaning. Students demonstrate their understanding of this unique poem format by either writing a reverso poem of their own or by performing two sides of an existing reverso.

Standards

K–2

- Uses prewriting strategies to plan written work

- Reads aloud familiar stories, poems, and passages with fluency and expression

3–5

- Uses prewriting strategies to plan written work

- Adjusts speed of reading to suit purpose and difficulty of the material

6–8

- Uses a variety of prewriting strategies

- Reads to interpret

Materials

- *Mirror Mirror: A Book of Reversible Verse* (2010) by Marilyn Singer *(optional)*

- *Reverso Sample* (page 160, reverso.pdf)

- *Reverse These Lines* (page 161, reversetheselines.pdf)

Preparation

Using a text such as *Mirror Mirror: A Book of Reversible Verse* by Marilyn Singer, familiarize yourself with the concept of reversos, which is a form of poetry that reverses the order of the lines in a poem. Additional ideas are provided in the Specific Grade Level Ideas.

Reversos *(cont.)*

Procedure

1. Explain to students that they will learn about a type of poem called a *reverso*. It is a poem with a unique format in which the poem can be read forward and backward with different meanings in either direction. Choose a poem from *Mirror Mirror: A Book of Reversible Verse* to share with students, or share *Reverso Sample* (page 160). Read the poem forward, which is the more conventional way of reading poetry. Ask, "Whose perspective is presented? What is the message of the poem?"

2. Then, read the reverse of the poem and discuss the same questions. Ask students what they notice about the format of a reverso poem. Discuss how the poet uses the same words but may change the punctuation, capitalization, and line breaks.

3. Share additional poems you have written or those from the book. Invite volunteers to read the two separate forward-and-back versions so that the two perspectives become clear.

4. Share suggestions for students about how to write a reverso poem. Marilyn Singer suggests that students "start with a few lines that can be flipped" and that can serve as the core idea for the poem. She also recommends working with a "lot of participles, infinitives, and single word sentences, as well as things that can be turned into questions and interjections." Discuss what these ideas mean and how students can use these suggestions to draft a reverso poem.

5. As a class, complete *Reverse These Lines* (page 161) to guide students in reversing lines so that the poem can be read forward and backward. Students in older grades may be able to draft forward and backward poems independently that have different meanings.

6. Give students a choice about how to further explore reversos. They may choose to write their own reverso poems or practice reading and presenting each view of the reverso poem.

7. Use the Questions for Discussion to debrief at the end of the lesson.

Reversos *(cont.)*

Questions for Discussion

- How do reversos present two sides to a story?

- How does punctuation affect the reading of the poem?

- How does capitalization affect the reading of the poem?

- How do line breaks affect the reading of the poem?

- Describe how you worked with language to create the poems.

- What were the challenges of writing a reverso poem?

Specific Grade Level Ideas

K–2

Have students focus on reading and comprehending the different perspectives, scenarios, and messages of the reversos and how punctuation, capitalization, and line breaks affect meaning and reading fluency. Begin by reading palindromes to show students how words such as *race car*, *pop*, *madam*, and *radar* have the same meaning when read backward and forward. Then, move to reversos, explaining that these poems can be read forward and backward for different meanings. Create an original reverso as a class.

3–5

Have students perform the different versions of the poems from *Mirror, Mirror: A Book of Reversible Verse* and discuss the differences in meaning, or have students write their own reversos, discussing the ways in which the meaning changes in either form. Extend this lesson by inviting students to change the meaning as the poem is read forward and backward and illustrate the two different perspectives.

6–8

Ask students to work from two different perspectives to create a reverso poem that captures the different vantage points.

Reverso Sample

Sample 1

To each his own—
Everything organized
Comforts me.
Chaos
Drives me crazy!

Drives me crazy!
Chaos
Comforts me.
Everything organized?
To each his own!

Sample 2

No comparison!
Summer sun and swimming?
It's the best time.
Fall coolness, falling leaves?
It's here again—
Already.

Already!
It's here again!
Fall coolness, falling leaves!
It's the best time.
Summer sun and swimming?
No comparison!

Name _____ Date _____

Reverse These Lines

Directions: Try writing a few lines. Then, reverse them. Play around with the punctuation. Does the meaning change? Does the new meaning make sense?

Draft your poem and put the lines in the appropriate spaces.

Forward	Backward

Storytelling

Storytelling

Understanding Storytelling

Storytelling has been part of every culture since the beginning of time (Norfolk, Stenson, and Williams 2006). Stories have been used to educate, to inspire, and to entertain. There is the story itself, and then there is the telling of the tale by a skilled teller. Storytellers use language, gesture, eye contact, tone, and inflection as they share a story with an audience. A good storyteller can create a sense of instant community among listeners as well as a deep connection with the material being explored (Hamilton and Weiss 2005). Because the storyteller interacts with the audience as the story is told, listeners often feel that they become part of the story world. They can even feel as if they are co-creators of the story when it is interactive, when connections with characters are developed, and when empathy is established. If you've ever heard a good storyteller tell a compelling story, you know it can transport you to another time and place.

In the following strategies, students benefit both from listening to stories and from becoming storytellers themselves. As listeners, students are supported in their visualization of the stories, which makes a narrative easier to both imagine and remember (Donovan and Pascale 2012). As storytellers, students develop additional skills, including skilled use of voice, improved verbal and nonverbal communication skills, and sense of pacing. Once stories are developed, you can also ask students to write them down, further enhancing their literacy skills.

When your students become storytellers, they fine-tune their communication skills. Oral fluency is developed as students explore vocal tone and inflection, pacing, sound effects, and the addition of rich sensory details to the telling. Listeners feel invited on a journey. Also, participating in the creation and telling of stories brings forward students' voices and their ideas.

Students find that stories provide vivid contexts that invite them into the world of the story. Characters are brought to life and interact with the audience through questions, eye contact, weaving a believable tale.

As students create, tell, and retell stories, they gain fluency in their communication skills, use of descriptive language, and persuasive abilities. They also expand their willingness to revisit, revise, and polish their work. By placing language arts in story settings, we provide a context that gives further meaning to language arts ideas and adds interest to the stories.

Storytelling (cont.)

Strategies for Storytelling

∞ Personification

Some people only use *personification* to refer to when we assign human qualities to inanimate objects or ideas and use the term *anthropomorphism* when we assign human qualities to animals. Other folks use these terms interchangeably. We will use *personification* to refer to all such assignment of human characteristics as it is most familiar to teachers and students, but feel free to use what best fits your curriculum. Personification is an ancient storytelling tool that continues today; think of both Aesop and the Toy Story movies (Cahill 2006). Stories that give animals and objects human traits allow listeners to think about their shortcomings in a safe way and invite us to think about moral or ethical values. When students personify elements of the natural world such as the sun in a nonfiction narrative, they explore nonfiction concepts from multiple perspectives. These tales engage learners and allow us to consider different perspectives. Because animals and objects take on human characteristics, the strategy also lends itself to figurative language.

∞ Exaggeration

It's human nature to exaggerate to make our stories more interesting. Often, we hear someone's story and have the desire to top it with something bigger, better, or more grandiose from our own treasure trove of experiences. Storytellers use exaggeration to emphasize their points and to pique the interest of their audiences. In fact, storyteller Jim Green identifies hyperbole as a tool in the storyteller's toolbox (Wohlberg 2012). Exaggeration also provides a way for students to explore unbelievable nonfiction facts.

In this strategy, exaggeration can be enhanced by the inclusion of incorrect language arts information, providing a vehicle for further developing students' understanding of language arts concepts. As in other techniques, embedding concepts related to language arts in a story allows students to experience a context in which knowledge of language arts is useful.

Storytelling (cont.)

The Untold Story

In this strategy, students are asked to consider the fact that every story is told from a particular perspective. In foregrounding one vantage point, the viewpoints of others are minimized, marginalized, or even left out. Perspective taking is critical to students' social development, and "understanding the perspective of others is an important skill that benefits children in their complex reasoning abilities that are important in math problems, such as story problems" (Heagle and Rehfeldt 2006, 32). The Untold Story strategy asks students to consider whose perspective is prominent in a story and what voices or concepts are missing. Inviting students to begin to look for the missing voices or ideas can develop critical thinking skills and empathy.

Retelling

Storytelling is an oral tradition that is grounded in telling and retelling stories. With each retelling, a story grows more polished, more dramatic, with clear high points and striking moments. Students become more responsive to working with listeners and more adept at using the storytelling process to spark the imagination of the audience. This revisiting of stories also strengthens students' writing skills as stories get honed and more richly detailed with each retelling.

Students can use the plot of a story as a flexible frame, improvising as the story unfolds. This builds comprehension skills and also allows students to feel free to adapt the stories based on the response of listeners, dwelling longer on a particular moment or adding embellishment when needed. This responsiveness heightens awareness of the role of an audience, which translates into writing.

Collaborative Storytelling

Collaborative storytelling often takes place in kids' play (Hourcade et al. 2002) and has been part of the cultural traditions of many families and communities (Coulter, Michael, and Poynor 2007). Students work together to build a story by adding short segments in their oral telling. Stories can be sparked by graphics, character traits, or settings. The story can be "passed" back and forth with each teller adding details and information before passing it on. A natural part of the process is a series of twists and turns that challenge students to maintain a shared story strand, keeping a clear logic so that the story remains together as it unfolds. This challenges them to listen attentively to the details and choices so that they can build on the unfolding events in meaningful and compelling ways by pivoting off details given, such as character traits, circumstance, and action. Students introduce obstacles and innovative solutions that take the characters on surprising journeys. Yew (2005) notes that constructing knowledge through the collective creation of narratives can provide more effective ways of learning in group settings than learning concepts individually.

Personification

Model Lesson: Nonfiction Literature

Model Lesson Overview

Students explore nonfiction literature that includes personification. They study the text as a model and retell the story through personification. As students explore the concept through storytelling, they deepen their understanding and view the concept through a different perspective. Students then choose a nonfiction concept and invent and tell stories of their own, using personification.

Standards

K–2

- Listens to and reads a variety of literary and informational texts and materials to gain knowledge and for pleasure

- Recites and responds to familiar stories, poems, and rhymes

3–5

- Understands the ways in which language is used in literary texts

- Makes basic oral presentations to the class

6–8

- Understands the use of language in literary works to convey mood, images, and meaning

- Uses appropriate verbal and nonverbal techniques for oral presentations

9–12

- Understands the effects of author's style and complex literary devices and techniques on the overall quality of a work

- Uses a variety of verbal and nonverbal techniques for presentations

Materials

- Nonfiction text that highlights personification

- *Character Development Planner* (page 172, characterplanner.pdf)

- Craft supplies to create props (paper, paint, or markers) *(optional)*

Personification *(cont.)*

Preparation

Decide how you will group students for this activity. Select an informational text in which the author uses personification, such as *Living Sunlight: How Plants Bring the Earth to Life* by Molly Bang and Penny Chisholm or *Ocean Sunlight: How Tiny Plants Feed the Seas* by Molly Bang and Penny Chisholm. Gather art supplies for students to use in creating props. Additional ideas are provided in the Specific Grade Level Ideas.

Procedure

1. Review the informational narrative text genre. Introduce the concept of storytelling by asking questions such as, "What is personification?" "Have you ever read a nonfiction book that is written as a narrative or a story?" "How might you bring nonfiction texts to life through storytelling?"

2. Read and discuss an informational narrative text in which something—an object, a plant, a natural force—is personified. Ask students to notice how the author uses personification to help bring the text to life in a unique way that shares a different perspective. Point out how the "character" talks and shows personality, perspective, and voice. Add students' ideas to a class chart for them to reference throughout the lesson.

3. Tell students that they will tell the story again, this time becoming a personified object, plant, natural force, etc. to help bring the story to life. Model how to come up with gestures to depict the story. Provide examples for students. Talk about how the living or nonliving object in the book would talk, behave, and move with human qualities.

4. Ask students to choose a living or nonliving object, plant, or natural force from the book that they will personify. Invite students to create and tell a story of the "character" within the context of the book. Note that they can tell the story from the perspective of the personified object as the narrator, or they can create a narrator that becomes the characters as the story unfolds. Distribute the *Character Development Planner* (page 172) and direct students to use it to help plan how they will personify their character through voice, movement, descriptive words, and point of view as they tell the story.

5. Allow time for students to create props, if desired.

6. Provide time for students to practice sharing information aloud about their characters. Once students feel comfortable, have them tell their stories to the class. Use the Questions for Discussion to debrief students. Encourage students to use descriptive detail, interactive moments, props, and voice to bring characters to life as the story is told.

Personification (cont.)

7. Have students write down their stories. Encourage students to include descriptive language as they describe their personified characters in writing. Ask students to share their written work with others.

Questions for Discussion

- What specific words helped you create a mental image?

- What descriptive language made for a compelling story?

- How did personification help you understand the nonfiction material?

- Describe the perspective of the character. What do we know about the character based on how the story is told?

- How do the pictures in the text provide additional information that adds to the creation of your story?

- How did the process of storytelling engage listeners?

- How did description work in developing the story?

Specific Grade Level Ideas

K–2

Explore the meaning of personification, using examples from familiar texts such as *Living Sunlight: How Plants Bring the Earth to Life* by Molly Bang and Penny Chisholm. Ask students, "Can the object talk in real life? Why do you think the author has the object tell the story?" As a class, create gestures, sounds, and movement for specific parts of the story. Reread excerpts to the class as they use these gestures, sounds, and movements in their own spaces at the same time. Choose an object, place, or thing from the classroom and personify it through storytelling. For example, explore the object's role in the classroom, how and why it got there, and its possible feelings, opinions, wishes, and thoughts.

Personification *(cont.)*

3–5

Students can incorporate the personification of more than one object or character into their storytelling. Ask students to consider how they can use their voice or simple gestures to depict different characters as they tell the story. Students can also read folklore such as myths, legends, folk tales, and fairy tales. They can use the strategy of personification to retell the story from the point of view of an inanimate object in the tale. Students can also invent their own stories and tell them using personification.

6–8

Have students incorporate other forms of figurative language, including hyperbole, simile, and metaphor, into the oral telling of their story. Explain to students that using these techniques will help them be more descriptive in their writing. Students can also brainstorm a list of occurences in nature, and then use personification to invent a story that explains why it occurs (e.g., why the ocean has waves).

9–12

Ask students to find their own examples of personification in both fiction and nonfiction texts, including narrative, poetry, and informational texts. Discuss the examples that students find, and have them discuss the ways in which the use of personification contributes to the overall reading experience and how it can be translated into storytelling.

Name _____   Date _____

Character Development Planner

Directions: Use this chart to plan how you will personify a nonfiction concept.

I plan to assign human qualities to the inanimate object or concept of:
Character traits:
Voice:
Props:
Gestures:

Exaggeration

Model Lesson: Two Truths and One Exaggeration

Model Lesson Overview

Storytellers have always used exaggeration to make stories more interesting, and having students recognize these embellishments is a critical skill. In this strategy, students will read an informational book and choose three interesting facts. Students will then create their own exaggerations of one of the facts and write short stories using those exaggerations. Peers will try to guess which one is the exaggeration. The art of storytelling helps students present their two truths and one exaggeration in a convincing manner.

Standards

K-2

- Reads nonfiction appropriate to grades K–2

- Uses prewriting strategies to plan written work

- Uses different voice level, phrasing, and intonation for different situations

3-5

- Reads nonfiction appropriate to grades 3–5

- Uses prewriting strategies to plan written work

- Uses a variety of verbal communication skills

6-8

- Reads nonfiction appropriate to grades 6–8

- Uses a variety of prewriting strategies

- Uses appropriate verbal and nonverbal techniques for oral presentations

Materials

- Various nonfiction texts appropriate to your grade level

- *Fact Collector* (page 176, factcollector.pdf)

- *Scenario Planner* (page 177, scenarioplanner.pdf)

- *Sample Storytelling Techniques* (page 178, storytellingtech.pdf)

Preparation

Gather nonfiction texts to be used in this lesson. Decide how to group students for this activity. Additional ideas are provided in the Specific Grade Level Ideas.

Exaggeration *(cont.)*

Procedure

1. Tell students that in order to fully appreciate nonfiction facts and be able to identify them, they are going to play "Two Truths and One Exaggeration." Then, tell students that they are going to find a fact and exaggerate it. Model this process by reading aloud the following fact from *Hottest, Coldest, Highest, Deepest* by Steve Jenkins: "The driest place is the Atacama Desert, in Chile, where no rain has fallen for the last 400 years." Ask students to help you create a scenario for this fact. For example, the scenario might be something like this:

> My mother was so tired of the snow and the icy winds last month, so she went online to research warm places for a vacation. She told my brother and me that she wanted a hot, dry place to escape the cold. "What about the Atacama Desert in Chile?" she asked with a chuckle in her voice. I shouted, "No! It hasn't rained there for the last 400 years!"

2. Explain that in this case, the fact is true, not exaggerated, and the scenario emphasizes the unbelievable nature of the fact. Tell students they should write similar scenarios for their facts so that readers will find it difficult to tell which facts are true and which fact is exaggerated.

3. Distribute the *Fact Collector* (page 176) to students. Help them select a nonfiction book. Students will read and study the book and locate three facts. Show students where they can record their facts, and explain that they will exaggerate one fact so that it is not entirely true. The exaggeration may make the information sound more interesting or unique, but it also makes the fact no longer true. Ask students to think about how they use storytelling techniques to tell a story about their fact in a way that feels true whether it is or is not.

4. Tell students that after recording two facts and an exaggeration, they will write scenarios like the example you shared, but their scenarios will be based on those three facts of information. Distribute the *Scenario Planner* (page 177), and allow time for students to write their scenarios, plan for their performances, and rehearse their storytelling. Share the *Sample Storytelling Techniques* (page 178) with students to help them with their storytelling. Remind students of the importance of voice and gesture in the development of characters and how they can create compelling moments through timing and sound effects.

5. Allow students to perform their scenarios as short stories through oral storytelling in small groups or as a class. The audience should guess which fact is exaggerated. Use the Questions for Discussion to debrief the activity.

Exaggeration (cont.)

Questions for Discussion

- What was convincing about the ways others told their stories?

- What storytelling techniques were used to tell the stories?

- As an audience member, how did you determine which facts were exaggerated and which were true?

- What choices did you make in your own storytelling? How did you make the true facts seem exaggerated? How did you disguise your exaggeration?

Specific Grade Level Ideas

K–2

Students can tell two stories with details: one with a true fact and one with the exaggeration. Encourage students to provide enough details and emotion in their storytelling so that listeners have trouble telling which happened and which did not. Model using familiar language in the stories that students can recognize from their own conversations, such as, "I ran so fast that I...," or, "I was so hungry that I thought I would...."

3–5

Students can complete the activity as written. Introduce the term *hyperbole*, and talk about how exaggeration can be used to create emphasis or effect in stories. Talk about the examples of hyperbole that have become common expressions in our casual speech, such as, "I've told you a million times," or, "I have a ton of homework."

6–8

Have students weave three scenarios into one well-crafted fiction or narrative nonfiction story. Discuss with students how including the exaggeration can change the plot, pace, or ending of the story. Discuss how exaggeration affects the telling of a story in terms of detail and description, emotional quality of the telling, pacing and use of silence, vocal intensity of the voice, and use of gesture. As students tell their stories in convincing ways, ask audience members to listen carefully to pick out the exaggeration.

Name _____ Date _____

Fact Collector

Directions: Use a nonfiction book to fill out the chart. Find two fascinating facts and record them in the chart with sketches and words. Then, find a third fact and exaggerate it.

Title of Book: _____

Fact #1	**Sketch**
_____ _____ _____ _____ _____	
Fact #2	**Sketch**
_____ _____ _____ _____	
Fact #3	**Exaggeration**
_____ _____ _____ _____	_____ _____ _____ _____

Name _____ Date _____

Scenario Planner

Directions: Write short scenarios for the facts and the exaggeration to help you plan for your performance.

Fact #1 Scenario

Storytelling Technique Ideas

Fact #2 Scenario

Storytelling Technique Ideas

Exaggeration Scenario

Storytelling Technique Ideas

Name _____ Date _____

Sample Storytelling Techniques

Find ways to engage the audience. Invite the audience into the story by posing a question.

Repeat lines to heighten audience awareness and add dramatic interest.

Allow your voice to hold emotion, reflecting the intensity of what is happening in the story as it unfolds.

Use facial expressions and eye contact to allow the audience to feel as though they were connected to the story.

Alter the tempo of your speech. Slowing down and speeding up language can intensify the story as the audience is brought along with the pace.

Use descriptive details to help the audience picture the story as it is being told.

The Untold Story

Model Lesson: Historical Fiction

Model Lesson Overview

In this strategy, students learn that stories are told from certain perspectives and that other voices or parts of the story are often minimized or left out as a result. The students hear an excerpt from a historical fiction text and record details about the setting and characters. They record specific words that allow them to visualize the story and connect with the emotions and perspectives of the character. Then, students create an imaginary diary entry, telling an untold story or presenting the perspective of another character.

Standards

K-2

- Reads and listens to a variety of texts for information and pleasure

- Plans and records improvisations based on personal experience and heritage, imagination, literature, and history

3-5

- Reads historical fiction appropriate to grades 3–5

- Plans and records improvisations based on personal experience and heritage, imagination, literature, and history

6-8

- Reads historical fiction appropriate to grades 6–8

- Creates improvisations and scripted scenes based on personal experience and heritage, imagination, literature, and history

9-12

- Reads a variety of literary texts

- Improvises, writes, and refines scripts based on personal experience and heritage, imagination, literature, and history

Materials

- Excerpts from a historical fiction text, such as books from the Dear America series

- *Diary Entry* (page 184, diaryentry.pdf)

- *Diary Samples* (pages 185–186, diarysamples.pdf) *(optional)*

The Untold Story (cont.)

Preparation

Find a historical fiction text that focuses on the point of view of one character but presents other characters for students to explore. Select one or more text excerpts from your chosen book to read aloud to students. Excerpts should be fairly short in length but include details of setting, action, and emotion, and should present at least one other character in addition to the main character. Excerpts written in the form of a diary are ideal. Decide if you will have students tell the untold story of an existing character in the scene or if they will create a new character for the scene. Additional ideas are provided in the Specific Grade Level Ideas.

Procedure

1. Ask students to consider a familiar story and think about whose point of view is left out. You can discuss point of view from well-known fairy tales, such as the witch's point of view in Hansel and Gretel, or the wolf's point of view in Little Red Riding Hood. Ask students to imagine what a different character might think or feel. Ask students, "How might exploring another character's untold story help us as readers? How might we better understand a story by thinking about the other sides of the story that remain untold?"

2. Show students the book you have selected. Tell students that this book is historical fiction because the author created parts of the story based on true events of history. The author may have fictionalized the characters, the settings, or the events of the book. Tell students that you are going to read a short section of the text to give them a sense of how this genre is structured.

3. Read the excerpt aloud. Then, during a second reading of the same excerpt, ask students to think about the important details they hear about the setting, characters, and events. Record ideas for students to reference throughout the lesson. Point out details that make the story unique, such as how a character uses words such as *'tis* or *'twas* in their speech.

4. Explain to students that one way for readers to deepen their understanding of a text is by imagining that they are a character in the story. Ask students to identify untold stories in the scene, such as the story from the point of view of another character or events that may be happening to another character as the story unfolds but are not described by the author. Tell students that they will choose a character and use the first-person point of view of "I" to become this character. Discuss how the writer brings stories to life with words.

5. Ask students to think about the stories we tell one another about funny events, scary moments, or memories we want to share as vividly as possible. Make a class list of these ideas for use in storytelling for students to reference throughout the lesson.

The Untold Story *(cont.)*

6. Keeping the events and details of the story as close as they can to the book, have students practice telling the story aloud from another character's point of view. Incorporate ideas discussed about how we tell stories aloud. Give students several opportunities to tell their stories orally in small groups.

7. Distribute *Diary Entry* (page 184) to students and have them write diary entries from the point of view of their chosen characters. If desired, read or provide students with *Diary Samples* (pages 185–186) as a guide. Use the Planning Questions to help support students as they work.

8. Once students have finished their final drafts, have them practice reading their diary entries with fluency and expression and storytelling techniques. If possible, record using available technology. Debrief, using the Questions for Discussion.

Planning Questions

- How do we bring stories to life in spoken words?

- How do we use voice, gestures, and sense of timing to convey a moment?

- When we are storytelling, how does the reaction of our listeners change the way we tell the story?

- How might we create an interactive moment with our audience to make them feel part of the story?

Questions for Discussion

- Which character's story did you tell, and why?

- What details from the original excerpt did you include? Why?

- What did you learn about this character?

- What did you learn about the relationship between this character and the main character?

- How did hearing the story performed change your understanding of or relationship to the story?

- What did you learn about a character by listening to your peers' untold stories?

- When did you find that you were connected to the story or the characters? What created this sense of connection?

The Untold Story *(cont.)*

Specific Grade Level Ideas

K–2

First, model the activity for the whole class. Choose an existing character in the story and tell the untold story as a class. Then, have students choose another character and try to depict—in words or pictures—how that character's perspective differs from what is shared in the story. Practice using different voices and gestures to depict a change in characters and reflect a character's personality.

3–5

Turn the activity into a whole-class exercise in which the class examines the story from every perspective. Each cooperative group should choose a character in the scene and tell the same set of events from that character's point of view. Encourage students to consider the language, movement, and characteristics of a character to portray their unique personality in the live moment of storytelling. Ask students to build on and embellish what they understand about the character from the text.

6–8

Invite students to invent a character that does not exist in the story but could have existed alongside the main character. Have them imagine the invented character's point of view and tell the untold story. Students can research authentic details of the historical background to inform their depiction of the character. Students can add a visual and audio component and tell the untold story through digital media or use the power of live storytelling with projected images on a whiteboard or screen behind them.

The Untold Story *(cont.)*

9–12

Students can use their research skills to dig deeper into another character's behavior, actions, or motives. Encourage students to look for the details about life in the era in which the historical fiction is set, and then include details in the story. These may be such things as how people dressed, how families were organized, what life was like for young children, what people did for fun, and how people spent time in their daily lives. Challenge students to bring historical details to life through the process of storytelling and creating a sense of the story world through the use of props, costume elements, and specific details to set the scene for the performed stories.

Name _____ Date _____

Diary Entry

Directions: Write a diary entry from the point of view of your chosen character.

Character _____

Date _____

Location _____

Dear Diary,

_____

_____

_____

_____

_____

_____

_____

_____

_____

_____

_____

_____

Diary Samples

Sample 1*

Me and Ma are packed and ready to go to America. We want to leave Ireland to have a better life. We will travel on a large boat to get to America. There will be lots of other people with us on the boat. They want a better life in America, too. Ma says it will be a long trip. I only get to pack one bag. I filled it with all of my clothes and a pair of shoes. I cannot bring any toys, but I do get to bring my journal. I will write about all of the things that happen on the trip. I am excited to go to America, and I am also a little scared. It will be a great adventure!

Sample 2

It was 1847 in Skibbereen, County Cork, Ireland. Ma and I agreed to send our youngest, Mary, to America to live with her aunt. Ma was helping Mary pack, and I sat in the chair with my pipe when it hit me. My youngest was leaving me, and life as we'd known it was over. I realized that 'twas no changing it. Mary would have to go to America to have a chance of a new life. When my Kate left, I had high hopes that we could join her over time, but knew 'twas unlikely. Kate was older and more sturdy of a girl for such a trip. Ma slowly packed her meager belongings, and sweet Mrs. Connelly quietly gave her oatmeal cakes and a hug for the travel with advice about dipping the cakes in tea to soften them during the long trip overseas. And all I could do was sit and think, puffing my pipe. 'Twas painful to talk about it. Sweet Mary seemed to be taking it all in stride, but I couldn't. I imagined walking over the fields and seeing the devastation to my crops from the blight. Black leaves. Withered stems. Diseased potatoes. All that work, plowing and sowing and praying—I realized 'twas bad, but to have Mary leaving for America. I just couldn't fathom it. 'Twas too much to bear. I sat there smoking my pipe, thinking of what I might say, but nothing came. Mary walked to me and pulled me back from my thinking. I grabbed her hand and she squeezed it and smiled. Tears came to my eyes.

*These samples are inspired by the historical fiction text *So Far From Home: The Diary of Mary Driscoll, an Irish Mill Girl, Lowell, Massachusetts, 1847* by Barry Denenberg.

Diary Samples *(cont.)*

Sample 3

In 1847, Mary departed for America after the blight killed off her Da's potato crop. Her sister had traveled to be with her aunt just months before, and now Mary's Ma was packing her belongings for a similar departure. It was the night before her ship sailed. Da was in the chair, quietly smoking. He barely moved. His eyes set on a fixed point out the window. From time to time, he sighed a long, slow sigh. His gaze never shifted. His clothes hadn't been changed since the day before, and the shadow of beard crept around his jaw. It was gray now after the long summer of worry and hard work. Puffs of smoke emerged regularly from his pipe, circled momentarily, and then floated upward. Mary watched him closely from across the room and then slowly walked toward him. He reached his hand out and grasped hers. She gave it a squeeze. Ma's voice broke the moment. Ma said, "'Tis a strange and far-off land." Da and Mary looked toward her for a moment, meeting her gaze. Then, Ma bent down to the tiny suitcase and continued packing with tears in her eyes. She snapped the buckles and placed it near the door. Mary leaned over and kissed her father, and then turned and went up the darkened stairs to bed to sleep. The journey would begin at dawn.

Retelling

Model Lesson: Folktales and Rich Cultural Histories

Model Lesson Overview

In this strategy, students work in small groups to practice the valuable skill of retelling. They choose from a collection of folktales inspired by different cultures. Students determine the most important aspects of the story and retell those parts, adding their own interpretation, language, voice, gestures, and props.

Standards

K–2

- Reads folktales appropriate to grades K–2
- Responds to familiar stories

3–5

- Reads folktales appropriate to grades 3–5
- Uses strategies to convey a clear main point when speaking

6–8

- Reads a variety of literary passages and texts
- Uses a clear point of view in oral presentations

Materials

- Grade-level appropriate folktales or myths
- *Retelling Plan* (page 191, retellingplan.pdf)

Preparation

Gather a collection of folktales from various cultures. Scan the texts or use the Internet to find additional information about the cultures represented in the folktales. Decide how students will research the culture by either gathering grade-level appropriate research materials or bookmarking helpful websites. Additional ideas are provided in the Specific Grade Level Ideas.

Retelling (cont.)

Procedure

1. Discuss with students how folktales have been told and retold over time and how stories have been passed orally from generation to generation. Ask students, "Do you think the details of the story stay the same each time they are retold, or do they change? Why?"

2. Explain that stories are retold across cultures for a variety of reasons—for entertainment, for education, to preserve history, to share tradition, to question, and to explain phenomena. Note that today, they are going to experience storytelling through the oral tradition. The basic elements of the story (plot, characters, setting) will stay the same, but the details will evolve with each retelling. Students will explore the power of storytelling to engage an audience through rich details, use of voice, gesture, sound effects, interaction with the audience, and sense of timing.

3. Choose one of the tales from the collection of folktales and share it with students. Review with students the background of the culture that is represented by the folktale. Discuss what you know about the culture, and with students, talk about how the culture is reflected in the tale.

4. As a group, practice retelling the main parts of the folktale. Discuss the skill of retelling and the importance of choosing the most important aspects of the tale to include. Retelling a story often means putting an individual spin on the tale as well. Remind students that the ways in which old folktales were shared in previous generations was by oral retelling. This retelling helps a story become more dramatic and polished.

5. Divide students into small groups. Explain that each group will choose one folktale to retell. Distribute the *Retelling Plan* (page 191) to groups and ask students to work together to reread the text and plan their retelling. Ask groups to consider what parts of the tale to include in retelling, what details to change or emphasize, what point of view to use, and how to interact with the audience.

6. Allow time for students to practice retelling their folktales. Remind them that it is all right to leave out some details in this type of retelling. The story is not fixed but shifts with each retelling. They should capture the essence of the story and use their own interpretation.

7. Have groups practice retelling with other small groups, and if appropriate, invite students to share with the whole class. Debrief the class, using the Questions for Discussion.

Retelling (cont.)

Questions for Discussion

- What happened to your story as you retold it again and again?

- What changed? What remained the same?

- What was most compelling as you listened and watched someone else tell his or her story?

- How did retelling your story several times affect you as a storyteller?

- What is the purpose of retelling stories orally?

- How might a folktale reveal aspects of the culture from which it came?

Specific Grade Level Ideas

K–2

As a whole class or in small groups, have students work together to retell the folktale. Talk as a group about the parts of the tale that are most important to include in the retelling and what kinds of storytelling techniques could bring the narrative and characters to life.

Students can use a graphic organizer that helps them summarize the beginning, middle, and end of the tale. As they retell, they can refer to these sequential plot points to help keep them on track. Use technology to record the retellings.

3–5

The activity can be used as an important writing experience. Encourage students to try different leads and storytelling techniques as they retell their stories. For example, what would the effect be if they were to begin their oral retelling with a question or by describing the setting? Use technology to record the retellings. How could sound effects help create the sense of setting? Have students work with character voice to include emotion as well as reveal character traits.

Retelling (cont.)

6–8

Have students retell the main events of myths, focusing on the use of literary devices such as foreshadowing and flashback. Also, have students consider the messages communicated in myths, and apply these ideas to today's society. Invite students to write an original myth or folktale to respond to a present-day issue and retell the story for others. Ask students to work on honing their sense of timing and the use of silence, pauses, and tone to heighten the emotional quality of a story. Use technology to record the retellings, and have students observe the evolution of their storytelling skills and techniques over time.

Name _____ Date _____

Retelling Plan

Directions: Work with your group to complete the chart and plan your retelling.

Folktale:	
What are the important parts of the story that we need to include in the retelling?	
What parts or details will we leave out?	
What details are worth developing further in our retelling?	
From what point of view will we tell the story?	
How will we interact with the audience?	
How will we introduce our story?	
What storytelling techniques can enhance the telling (use of voice, gesture, sound effects, timing, props, costume)?	

Collaborative Storytelling

Model Lesson: The Twisting and Turning Plot

Model Lesson Overview

In this strategy, students work together and collaborate to tell and then write a story with a twisting and turning plot told from two vantage points. They deepen their understanding of the story elements of fiction: characters, problem, solution, setting, and theme.

Standards

K–2

- Makes contributions in class discussions

- Knows setting, main characters, main events, sequence, narrator, and problems in stories

- Uses different voice level, phrasing, and intonation for different situations

3–5

- Responds to questions and comments

- Understands elements of character development

- Makes basic oral presentations to the class

6–8

- Understands elements of character development

- Makes oral presentations to the class

- Uses appropriate verbal and nonverbal techniques for oral presentations

Materials

- Text with two narrators

- *The Plot Twister* (page 196, plot.pdf)

- Art supplies for making props (paper, paint, or markers)

Preparation

Locate a text with two different narrators, such as *Once Upon a Cool Motorcycle Dude* by Kevin O'Malley or *The Wanderer* by Sharon Creech. Additional ideas are provided in the Specific Grade Level Ideas.

Collaborative Storytelling *(cont.)*

Procedure

1. Review the main story elements of fiction with students: characters, problem, solution, setting, and theme.

2. Have students stand in a circle. Tell them that they will create a story collaboratively. Explain that you will begin the story and you will pass the telling on to the next person. When that person gets the story, he or she will add a little more and pass it along to the next person in the circle. Remind students that a good story has central characters and events that advance the plot in a way that makes sense.

3. Begin with a compelling lead such as, "Imagine being lost in the woods and you only have a…." Turn to the student next to you, and invite him or her to continue. When the story has made its way around the circle, ask students what worked and what didn't and how they might make the story better if they were to revisit it. Ask students to use the elements of oral storytelling, including spoken words, sound effects, gesture, and movement that help bring the story to life and establish the characters.

4. Explain to students that two or more people can draft a story by sharing ideas and including different elements of a story. Tell students that one way this can be done is for each author to share parts of a story from a certain perspective and then interweave those two points of view, thereby creating a story with two narrators. Tell students this is the kind of collaborative storytelling that they are going to practice today.

5. Share an excerpt from the text you selected with two narrators. You may also consider sharing an image and asking students to tell a story about the image from different character perspectives. Talk as a class about the narrators, what they do and say in the text, how they compare to each other, and how they offer different points of view.

6. Place students in pairs. Tell them that each pair will create two new characters and tell a combined story that includes information and perspectives from each character. It will be a story with two narrators. Distribute *The Plot Twister* (page 196) to each pair and direct them to use it to reflect on their own ideas for a story. Remind students that the events of the story, though told from two points of view, must incorporate both narrators in some way that makes sense.

7. Direct students to use the notes they take on *The Plot Twister* to plan how to orally tell a story about their created characters in which the plot twists and turns. Give pairs the opportunity to perform their stories again and again to different peers.

Collaborative Storytelling (cont.)

8. Assist students as they write and illustrate their stories. Then, give students the opportunity to create props and act their stories out for an audience.

9. Discuss the process with students, using the Questions for Discussion.

Questions for Discussion

- Describe your story's characters, problem, solution, setting, and theme.

- How did your story's plot twist and turn? Why?

- How does each character approach the storytelling when it's his or her turn?

- What elements of storytelling were used, such as embellishment of details, sounds, voice, gesture, and props?

- What did you notice about your experience of the story as you listened?

- How does one character's story intertwine with the other's?

- Describe your experience working collaboratively to write a story.

- How did your story change after telling it a few different times?

- As you listened to or told stories, what made the storytelling compelling?

Specific Grade Level Ideas

K–2

Students can work together to map out plots that incorporate two different characters and perspectives. Encourage students to improvise the stories, adding details about characters and events as they go. They can then explore their tales in writing. You can time each partner and allow him or her to start the story, and when the time is up, have the other partner take over, beginning where the story left off. Students can work from paintings, photographs, special objects, etc., to inspire a story.

3–5

The activity can be used as written. Students can also use collaborative storytelling for retelling information they've heard in a nonfiction text, perhaps by sharing chronological facts that describe an important event, biography, or historical concept. Consider how the storytelling process can be woven together between tellers with a seamless quality.

Collaborative Storytelling *(cont.)*

6–8

Have students further explore the use of more than one narrator. Help students find books that include various narrators or points of view and have them compare and contrast these different perspectives. Ask students to develop storytelling strategies for differentiating the narrator from other speakers in the story.

Name _____ Date _____

The Plot Twister

Directions: Work with your partner. Use the graphic organizer to plan your story together. Make sure your events relate to each other.

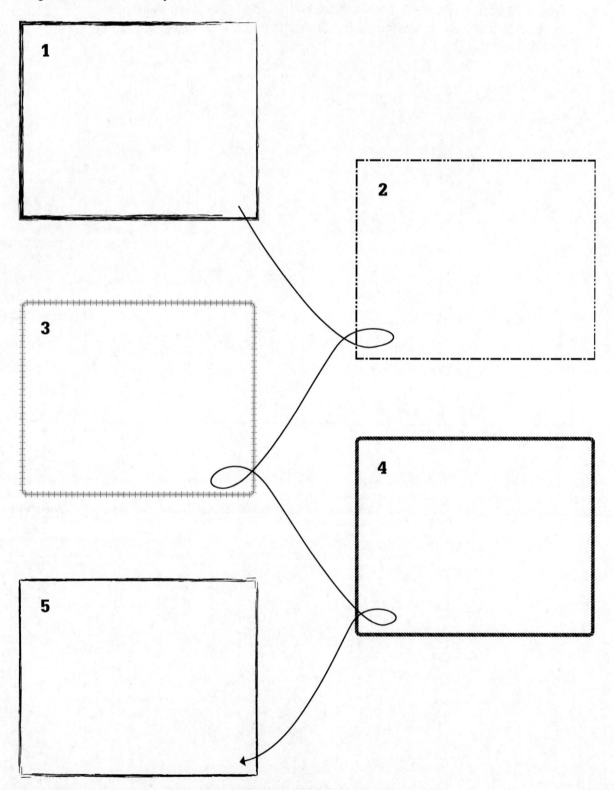

Visual Arts

Visual Arts

Understanding Visual Arts

The importance of images and visual media in contemporary culture is changing what it means to be literate in the 21st century. Today's society is highly visual, and visual imagery is no longer supplemental to other forms of information. New digital technologies have made it possible for almost anyone to create and share visual media. Yet the pervasiveness of images and visual media does not necessarily mean that individuals are able to critically view, use, and produce visual content. Individuals must develop these essential skills in order to engage capably in a visually-oriented society. Visual literacy empowers individuals to participate fully in a visual culture.

—Association of College & Research Libraries (2011)

We are bombarded with images on a daily basis, and though we have become more skilled at reading the nontextual representation of ideas, our visual-literacy abilities need to develop further. Why then, is education so often text based? Working with images can provide opportunities for students to observe, notice details, and make meaning. Visual work can communicate nuances that words cannot. In this section, we see how students can use visual art as a language that is more unstructured than text.

Particular to visual arts is hands-on work with various materials. Visual artists use their art in many ways—to create narratives, observe, explore patterns, translate, represent, and juxtapose ideas using visual communication. Using the elements of art—*line, form, shape, color, texture,* and *pattern*—students can investigate and create visual representations of ideas. They can also create images as a way to tell what they know.

When students process visual information as well as verbal, they are using different parts of the brain. Allan Paivio suggests that learning can be expanded by the inclusion of visual imagery, allowing students what he termed "dual coding" (quoted in Reed 2010). All curricular areas have visual aspects, so providing students with the opportunity to work with multiple representations of content is easy to incorporate and will allow students new ways to engage in and access ideas related to language arts.

Visual Arts (cont.)

Strategies for Visual Arts

ᔥ Visual Narrative

In this strategy, students create and arrange images in sequence to tell a story or create a narrative. The story can be told through images alone, or the pictures can interact with text. Students' understanding of curricular content is enhanced as they create visual narratives that demonstrate and/or apply their learning. Often, creating a visual narrative makes it easier for students to grasp connections and clarify their thinking, which they can then translate into text. Students can illustrate concepts related to language arts, translating their understanding into visual form.

Visual narratives can culminate in the creation of simple books, digital image essays, magazines, storyboards, comics, and other formats that are easy to make and allow students to compose content and apply and articulate their knowledge in new ways. Teaching artist and researcher Wendy Strauch-Nelson (2011) notes that students "seemed drawn to the complementary relationship between the linear style of words and the layered nature of images" (9).

ᔥ Visual Patterns

Artists often work with patterns. *Pattern* is considered one of the fundamental communication elements in the visual-arts principles of design. These design elements include *line, shape, form, texture, pattern*, and *color*. Through the visual arts, students can demonstrate a variety of curricular concepts by creating and manipulating patterns. Working with patterns can guide observations, and shifting patterns can generate interest and curiosity. Illustrators use their understanding of these elements to deepen meaning and enhance the relationships between text and image. Often, images in books tell a compelling story of their own that can deepen the themes of a text.

ᔥ Representation

Students investigate the ability of the visual arts to communicate information and ideas in compelling ways, to direct our attention, and to add layers of meaning. When students investigate the visual arts through the creation of a graphic novel, they translate their understanding of events, characters, setting, and other elements into new forms, taking ownership of ideas and engaging with symbolism and metaphor. Weaving together text and image in compelling ways allows students to consider the relationship between image and text and how they work together to enhance meaning.

Visual Arts (cont.)

Mixed Media

This strategy allows students to experiment with putting a range of materials together in new ways. Students manipulate materials, experiment with the juxtaposition of materials, and create two- or three-dimensional pieces such as mobiles, collages, assemblages, dioramas, and digital installations. This process allows students to use metaphors, prompting them to make meaning of experiences in new ways and boil concepts down to their essence to consider qualities rather than literal representations. Students test and explore ideas in experiential, hands-on ways; make choices about how they will use materials to communicate; and explore cause-and-effect relationships in the process of working with different media. The use of multiple representations is essential to the development of flexible thinking in language arts. This interpretive exploration will draw other themes. The construction of three-dimensional pieces requires students to interpret and explore ideas visually.

Transformation

In this strategy, students transform found materials such as books, images, posters, record album covers, and other found items into new forms. Students work with a variety of media and found materials to give new life and new meaning through the translation of their ideas in the creative process. In the process, the appearance of the materials and the meaning is altered. Repurposing, recycling, and reinterpreting materials provide students with rich ways to access curricular ideas and bring their ideas to life. Through artwork, students transform the meaning of the words on a page, in an article, or throughout a discarded book. They discover how words and visuals work together to communicate new meaning and reflect on the process of altering the meaning and the message of words.

Visual Narrative

Model Lesson: Digital Storytelling

Model Lesson Overview

In this strategy, students choose a final draft from their writing folders and publish it as a digital story. As part of the process, each student creates a storyboard and decides how to break up the writing piece into meaningful scenes that are properly sequenced. Students explore how text, images, and sound work together to create meaning.

Standards

K–2	3–5
• Uses technology to publish work appropriate to grades K–2 • Selects prospective ideas for works of art	• Uses technology to publish work appropriate to grades 3–5 • Selects prospective ideas for works of art

6–8	9–12
• Uses technology to publish work appropriate to grades 6–8 • Understands how symbols, images, sound, and other conventions are used in visual media	• Uses technology to publish work appropriate to grades 9–12 • Applies various subjects, symbols, and ideas in one's artworks

Materials

- Example of visual narrative (comic, graphic novel, storyboard)
- *Digital Story Planning Guide* (page 206, digitalstory.pdf)
- Art supplies (markers, crayons, paint, clay, scissors, glue, etc.)
- *Storyboard Planner* (page 207, storyboard.pdf)
- Software for digital storytelling, such as iMovie®, Microsoft Movie Maker®, or Microsoft® Photo Story

Preparation

Identify an example of visual narrative to share with students such as a comic strip or book, a graphic novel, or a storyboard. Do an online search for examples of student digital stories. Additional ideas are provided in the Specific Grade Level Ideas. Explore iMovie® or other digital storytelling resources, and choose one suitable for your students to use to publish their work.

Visual Narrative *(cont.)*

Procedure

1. Explain that a visual narrative is a story told in a sequence of images that are often linked with text. Share the example of a visual narrative that you chose, and discuss how the artist may have decided to break the story or information into panels and how he or she sequenced the panels.

2. Tell students that they will be creating a storyboard to help them publish a written story as a digital story. Have students select one of their final drafts from their writing folders for this activity. Photocopy student writing pieces so that they can cut them into meaningful parts. Distribute either the *Digital Story Planning Guide* (page 206) or the *Storyboard Planner* (page 207), whichever best suits students' needs, to students, and have them begin thinking about the images for their stories.

3. With students, use the visual narrative you have shared to point out how the story was broken up. Tell students that they will decide how to break up their own stories into sections. Help students do this by asking questions such as, "What is the most important information?" "What sequence makes sense?"

4. Tell students to each cut the photocopied story apart and glue each section onto the storyboard planner of choice.

5. Talk as a class about how illustrations can help make each section more meaningful. Continue to use your visual narrative example to point out how the illustrations work well with the text. Use the Planning Questions to guide students' thinking.

6. Have students review their planning storyboards to evaluate how well they conveyed the story and edit or add visual detail as necessary.

7. Allow students time to use the chosen software to create their digital stories. Students should use the *Digital Story Planning Guide* to support them during this work. Then, have students practice rereading their completed digital stories aloud for fluency.

8. Provide time for students to share their work with one another.

9. Have students discuss the process of making their visual narratives using the Questions for Discussion.

10. Ask students to create an author/illustrator statement, detailing the choices made in the creation of the digital story.

Visual Narrative *(cont.)*

Planning Questions

- How will you break your story up into meaningful parts?

- What images can you create to help tell your story?

- What medium will you choose to create your artwork and why (colored pencils or paint, photographs, drawing programs on a computer)?

Questions for Discussion

- How did you choose your visual images?

- How did the images you used influence the text?

- How did your pictures and text work together?

- What did you learn about storytelling from creating your storyboard?

- As you were reading and viewing the work of others, what did you realize about visual narratives?

Specific Grade Level Ideas

K–2

Have students create their artwork first and then write the text for each image. The storyboard can be a large piece of butcher paper with boxes for the artwork and space beneath for the text. Use a digital camera to photograph students' pictures and upload them into the video-editing software of your choice. Create a class digital story in which each student writes and creates one piece of artwork as part of the larger story.

3–5

Have students flag two revisions they made to their drafts while working on their storyboards. Students can also create movie trailers in which they recommend a book through digital storytelling, previewing highlights about the story and images. You can find examples of movie trailers online.

Visual Narrative *(cont.)*

6–8

Invite students to explore additional content through digital storytelling, using such topics as mythology, state parks, buildings, or astronomy. Students can also create movie trailers to recommend books to others. Have students move between the creation of images and the writing of text, adding details to both modes of communication as they proceed.

9–12

In addition to the 6–8 Specific Grade Level Ideas, students can handle more sophisticated software for publishing digital stories. They can also use webcams to film introductions to the project or to film short discussions on the process they used to create the storyboards.

Name _____ Date _____

Digital Story Planning Guide

Directions: Use the chart to help plan for your digital story.

Author: _____ Date: _____ Title: _____	

Sketch the photo, illustration, transition, or title that will show during the narration on this page.	Media List: Check the boxes to show your choice.
	☐ I will take my own photo.
	☐ I will use paint, clay, crayons, or another medium.
	☐ I will create a picture on the computer.
	☐ Other: _____

Narration:

_____

_____

_____

_____

_____

_____

(from Bogard and McMackin 2012)

Name _____   Date _____

Storyboard Planner

Directions: Plan your scenes using the storyboard.

Text	Sketch

Visual Patterns

Model Lesson: Signature Characteristics

Model Lesson Overview

Students choose an illustrator and analyze the artist's use of design elements, including line, shape, form, texture, pattern, and color throughout his or her work. After identifying how illustrators have specific patterns in their work, students illustrate their own writing, paying attention to the elements of line, shape, form, texture, and color.

Standards

K–2

- Relates new information to prior knowledge and experience

- Uses visual structures and functions of art to communicate ideas

3–5

- Uses prior knowledge and experience to understand and respond to new information

- Uses visual structures and functions of art to communicate ideas

6–8

- Uses new information to adjust and extend personal knowledge base

- Knows some of the effects of various visual structures and functions of art

Materials

- Books featuring illustrations that highlight design elements

- *Finding Patterns* (pages 211–212, patterns.pdf)

Preparation

Gather a collection of books that feature multiple works of one or more illustrators if possible. You may want to draw from illustrator awards such as the Pura Belpré Award, or go to the American Library Association website (http://www.ala.org) to find more. Additional ideas are provided in the Specific Grade Level Ideas.

Visual Patterns *(cont.)*

Procedure

1. Begin by asking students to think about the illustrations they have created in the past. Ask, "Where did you get your inspiration as illustrators? Where do you think artists get their inspiration as illustrators?" Discuss illustrators whom students are familiar with and who have a unique style that is easily recognizable. Have students share a time when they were able to identify a particular illustrator's work.

2. Display *Finding Patterns* (pages 211–212) for students to see. Share one of the books you have gathered, and focus on the illustrations as you examine it as a class. Then, record the six design elements that students are focusing on for them to reference throughout the lesson: color, line, shape, form, texture, and pattern. As a class, discuss the questions from *Finding Patterns* to examine how these elements can be found and analyzed in illustrations.

3. Divide students into small groups. Have each group choose an illustration from the books you have provided. Provide each student with a copy of *Finding Patterns*. Have students work within their small groups to discuss the design elements within the illustration and complete *Finding Patterns*. Offer assistance as needed.

4. Have each group share their findings with the class and display the illustration for students to observe.

5. Invite students to illustrate their own writing pieces, using their interpretation of the design elements of line, shape, form, pattern, texture, and color.

6. Debrief, using the Questions for Discussion.

Questions for Discussion

- What are some "signature" characteristics of each artist's approach?

- How do the pictures and words interact to convey meaning?

- How do pictures convey messages? Discuss an example.

- What elements of line, shape, form, pattern, texture, and color did you use in your own illustrations, and why?

Visual Patterns (cont.)

Specific Grade Level Ideas

K–2

Conduct an illustrator study as a class. Include works that recognize many cultures such as those from the Coretta Scott King Award and the Pura Belpré Illustrator Award. Have students try out the illustrator's style in their own illustrations. They can do this by creating an additional page for the book and adding text and images. You may also focus on the color of the illustrations. In order for students to better understand how colors reveal mood or create feeling, read aloud *The Way I Feel* by Janan Cain. Have students discuss their artistic choices.

3–5

In addition to the K–2 Specific Grade Level Ideas, invite students to create their own books by adding their own artistic flair while borrowing from the illustrator's style and focusing on the message that the illustrations convey. Students can write an artist's statement that discusses their approach to the illustrations. Also, consider reading one excerpt at a time from *Show Me a Story! Why Picture Books Matter: Conversations with 21 of the World's Most Celebrated Illustrators* by Leonard S. Marcus in order to provide students with the insights of multiple illustrators whose work they may already know.

6–8

Invite students to examine the social themes that motivate and inspire the artists of various cultures. Students can also choose another book that they feel demonstrates criteria for an award, such as the Pura Belpré Illustrator Award, and write persuasive essays to compete for the award themselves based on criteria from a real or imagined review board.

Name _____ Date _____

Finding Patterns

Directions: Look at the illustrations in a book. Then, answer the questions.

Title of book and name of illustrator:						
Color Describe the colors in the illustration. What color choices did the artist make? How does he or she communicate mood?	**Line** How would you describe the artist's use of line in the illustration (thickness; type of medium used, such as ink, charcoal, brush stroke; quality of line, such as hard or soft)?	**Pattern** Describe a visual pattern you notice in the colors or designs.	**Shape** What shapes are found in the illustration?	**Form** How is the illustration bordered or framed? How are the elements in the illustration arranged into a composition that hangs together?	**Texture** What materials do you think the illustrator used for texture in the illustrations?	

Finding Patterns *(cont.)*

1. How do the illustrations tell the story?

_____

_____

_____

_____

_____

_____

_____

_____

2. What is the theme or overall message of the book?

_____

_____

_____

_____

_____

_____

_____

_____

_____

Representation

Model Lesson: Graphic Novels

Model Lesson Overview

Students explore how graphic novels represent stories visually and how readers gather multiple layers of meaning by "reading" the visuals and the text. Students take part in a graphic novel hunt in which they interact with the text. They add sticky notes to mark specific ways in which the visuals and text communicate meaning, and they create their own dialogue and additional scenes with pictures and words. Finally, students choose a short poem, a nursery rhyme, a page or two from a book, or a writing piece from their writer's notebooks, and represent the text in the format of a graphic novel.

Standards

K–2
- Knows how different elements help to establish plot, setting, and character in visual narratives
- Knows various purposes for creating works of visual art

3–5
- Understands different messages conveyed through visual media
- Knows various purposes for creating works of visual art

6–8
- Understands a variety of messages conveyed by visual media
- Distinguishes among multiple purposes for creating works of visual art

9–12
- Uses a range of strategies to interpret visual media
- Identifies intentions of those creating artworks

Materials

- Collection of graphic novels
- *Graphic Novel Hunt* (page 218, novelhunt.pdf)
- Sticky notes
- Large paper
- *Graphic Novel Templates* (pages 219–221, noveltemplate.pdf)

Representation *(cont.)*

Preparation

Gather a collection of graphic novels. Select one graphic novel to use in direct instruction and preview it before sharing with the class. Display the pages of the graphic novel for students to see or gather multiple copies of the chosen graphic novel so that students can carefully examine the visuals as you share. *There's a Princess in the Palace* by Zoe B. Alley is large in size and allows for easy viewing. Familiarize yourself with the *Graphic Novel Hunt* (page 218) in order to model the way that students will interact with the graphic novels. Additional ideas are provided in the Specific Grade Level Ideas.

Procedure

1. Ask students to share what they know about graphic novels and what experiences they have had with reading them. Explain to students that when they read a graphic novel, they "read" the pictures and the words in order to fully understand all of the layers of the story. Tell students that many stories are represented visually and with text.

2. Share an excerpt from a graphic novel with students. Display the images for students to see, or provide them with their own copies. As you share the book, choose a few examples to model from the *Graphic Novel Hunt* (page 218). Discuss the choices made by the author and illustrator in presenting the book in this format. Use the Questions for Discussion to help you.

3. Tell students that they are going to use sticky notes to interact with the text, to point out features of the pictures and story, to add visuals, and to add text. Model how to use sticky notes as directed on *Graphic Novel Hunt*. As a class, find a place to add an additional scene. Model how to sketch or write the scene on a sticky note, and carefully stick it to the part of the text where the scene extends meaning.

4. Distribute *Graphic Novel Hunt* to students and allow them to choose to work alone, in pairs, or in small groups to explore a graphic novel from the collection you have shared with students.

5. Have students share their findings with the whole class.

Representation *(cont.)*

6. Invite students to choose a short poem, a nursery rhyme, a page or two of a book, or a writing piece from their own folders. Tell students that they will represent the text in the format of a graphic novel. If desired, provide students with large paper and let them decide how to create boxes or circles for their visuals and text, or distribute the *Graphic Novel Templates* (pages 219–221) for students to use to help them plan their stories and how they will organize their pictures and texts.

7. After students are finished with their graphic novels, have them share their finished work with the class.

Planning Questions

- What illustrations can you use to work with the text?

- What images will tell the story or add to the story being told?

- How will you frame your images to help the viewer focus their attention?

Questions for Discussion

- How would you describe the characteristics of the graphic novel (style, use of color, suggestion of mood)?

- How are the stories sequenced (action, change of location, etc.)?

- Why do you think the author made these choices?

- What do the images communicate that the text does not?

- How do the images work with the text?

- What did the opportunity to "read" the visuals along with the text do for your understanding of the story?

Representation *(cont.)*

Specific Grade Level Ideas

K–2

Have students choose one or two lines from a familiar read-aloud to start. Have students try their hand at creating illustrations for the lines of text or an untold part of the story that is only shown through a picture. Remind students that illustrators often make their pictures extend slightly beyond the boundary of boxes, or have the box cut off part of the scene or character. The pictures do not have to fit neatly inside the box. Then, challenge students to create speech bubbles for dialogue. Discuss how colors communicate mood and whether they would like their illustrations to be realistic or unrealistic.

3–5

Extend this activity by teaching students about the different types of leads that authors use. Point out how an author can craft interesting leads by asking a question, showing action, or getting right to the point of a story and engaging readers immediately. Invite students to create different leads for fairy tales and represent the leads visually and with text. Ask students to create an image that serves as a visual lead-in to the story. Experiment with telling the story through image first, adding text and working to create illustrations from text.

6–8

Students can explore how a particular cartoonist uses similar craft strategies to tell different stories in visual ways.

Students should also hunt for the presence of stereotypes in graphic novels by examining clothing, dialogue, gender roles, and other details. Invite students to write revisions without the stereotypes and discuss the changes. Ask students to identify an episode from their own lives or select a significant moment from a nonfiction text and move this writing into the form of a graphic novel. Discuss how working with ideas from real life influences the choices made in depiction of characters and events. Create visuals that illustrate literary devices such as metaphor or onomatopoeia.

Representation *(cont.)*

9–12

In addition to the 6–8 Specific Grade Level Ideas, students can find stories that are depicted in graphic novels but are also told in more traditional written form. Students can then compare and contrast how the format of a text influences the story and the reading experience and how the inclusion of images can tell a story and add detail, contrast, or humor to a text.

Name _____ Date _____

Graphic Novel Hunt

Directions: Complete the checklist to explore a graphic novel. Use sticky notes to explore each item.

☐ Find a picture that tells a story without words. Write a line or two of text for it.

☐ Find a place in which words *and* pictures show a character's feelings. Label it *Feelings*.

☐ Find a place where only the picture shows the character's feelings (facial expression or body language). Add words to describe what the character might be thinking or feeling.

☐ Find a place to add dialogue to a picture. Write the dialogue on a sticky note.

☐ Find a place where the pictures show humor. Write what the illustrator does to show humor.

☐ Find a place where the setting or mood is shown visually. Label it *Setting*.

☐ Find a place where you could add another scene to the story. Sketch a picture, or write words.

☐ Find a place where a sound word, or *onomatopoeia,* would deepen meaning. Write the sound word you would use.

☐ Find a place where the illustrations extend beyond the boundary of the boxes.

Name _____   Date _____

Graphic Novel Templates

Directions: Use the templates to help plan your story and organize your pictures and text.

Name _____ Date _____

Graphic Novel Templates *(cont.)*

Name _____   Date _____

Graphic Novel Templates *(cont.)*

Mixed Media

Model Lesson: Life Stories Told and Retold

Model Lesson Overview

Students listen to a story that explores memory and how people retell the events of their own lives. Students interview an elder or a family member and represent the essence of his or her life through the careful composition of found objects. They create a sculpture out of the assembled items called an *assemblage*.

Standards

K–2

- Asks and responds to questions

- Knows how different media, techniques, and processes are used to communicate ideas, experiences, and stories

3–5

- Responds to questions and comments

- Knows how different media, techniques, and processes are used to communicate ideas, experiences, and stories

6–8

- Asks questions to seek elaboration and clarification of ideas

- Knows how the qualities and characteristics of art media, techniques, and processes can be used to enhance communication of experiences and ideas

Materials

- Book that retells a character's life events

- *Creating Interview Questions* (page 226, questions.pdf)

- Images of assemblages from the Internet

- Various found objects that may represent life stories

- *Mixed Media Catalog* (page 227, mixedmedia.pdf)

Mixed Media *(cont.)*

Preparation

Select a book that features a retelling of life events, such as *Grandpa Green* by Lane Smith. Familiarize yourself with *Creating Interview Questions* (page 226), and make one copy for each student. Decide if you will supply students with materials for making assemblages or if you would like them to use found objects. Conduct an Internet search to find images of assemblages created by a range of artists such as Louise Nevelson, Joseph Cornell, Wolf Vostell, and Picasso to share with students. Additional ideas are provided in the Specific Grade Level Ideas.

Procedure

1. Ask students to remember a special time in their own lives. What is a memory of the event, and how has the memory changed over time? How did the event make them feel? Why do they think they still remember this event? What makes some life events more memorable than others?

2. Share a story that features a retelling of life events. Discuss with students the events in the story that were important in the character's life.

3. Tell students that they will have the opportunity to represent the important parts of a loved one's life through a type of visual art called an assemblage. Share examples that you have gathered. Explain to students that an *assemblage* is a form of visual arts in which the artwork is created by putting together found objects to communicate about a story or memory.

4. Ask students how they might find out about the important parts of someone's life. Lead students to the conclusion that interviews are a great way to gather firsthand knowledge about a person's life experiences. Discuss how interviews work. Distribute copies of *Creating Interview Questions* (page 226) to students. As a class, review the interview tips and then help students draft questions. Tell students they will conduct interviews for homework.

5. Once interviews are complete, discuss how students could represent the ideas in the interviews through actual artifacts or objects that symbolically represent significant life moments. Ask students to identify and collect a variety of artifacts and found objects that represent themes that emerged from their interviews. If collected, share the found objects you have gathered and allow students to use those as well.

6. Once they've collected a range of objects, distribute the *Mixed Media Catalog* (page 227) to students. Have students record the objects they are using and write about the big ideas behind these objects.

Mixed Media *(cont.)*

7. Students are ready to use the found objects to experiment with creating a two- or three-dimensional composition. This can be a collage, a sculpture, or a composed collection of objects presented in a way that feels representative of ideas being conveyed.

8. Have students write short artist statements about their assemblages. What meaning does the piece hold for the artist? What is important to communicate? Allow time for students to present their work to the class.

9. Debrief, using the Questions for Discussion.

Questions for Discussion

- What objects are included in each piece?

- How did you select the objects for the assemblage?

- How do the objects and composition of the piece reflect themes from the interview?

- What moments were represented—big life-changing events or small but significant moments?

- What similarities and differences do you see in the ideas selected?

- What artistic choices were made in each assemblage, including the objects selected, the composition of the piece, and how the assemblage was created to communicate ideas from the interviews?

Specific Grade Level Ideas

K–2

Students should work in small groups with you. Make sure to send home relevant information about this lesson and activity so that family members can help facilitate and participate in the interview.

As a class, conduct a genre study and gather additional books with the theme of bonding with grandparents, such as *The Hello Goodbye Window* by Norton Juster.

Mixed Media *(cont.)*

3–5

Explore the genre of biography and have students write a biography to accompany the assemblage they have created for the person they interviewed. Discuss how life stories can be shared through words or visually through art. What artistic choices can they include to show the idea of a life over time?

Invite students to capture a scene from a favorite book, song, poem, or play, or have them capture the essence of their own writing by representing it through found objects that are composed into an assemblage.

6–8

Have students further investigate the practice of conducting an interview. Discuss the ethics involved, and have students write consent forms before interviewing their participants. If the participant gives consent to be recorded, students can explore the use of technology tools to record their interview and transcribe the data.

Students can also investigate memoir, write a memoir, and then create an assemblage that captures aspects of their own lives.

Name _____   Date _____

Creating Interview Questions

Directions: Read the Interview Tips before you begin the interview. Write four or more interview questions that you want to ask.

Interview Tips

- Try not to ask questions with *Yes* or *No* answers. Ask open-ended questions beginning with words such as *how*, *when*, *why*, and *what*.

- Ask questions about the different stages of your subject's life, such as childhood and adulthood.

- Ask about feelings such as times when your subject was surprised, thrilled, sad, etc.

- Ask about the different roles a person has played in your subject's life (artist, mother, friend, etc.).

- Ask about important moments such as turning points, signature moments, and cherished memories.

1. _____

_____

_____

2. _____

_____

_____

3. _____

_____

_____

4. _____

_____

_____

Name _____ Date _____

Mixed Media Catalog

Directions: Look at the found objects for your project. Complete the chart.

	Describe the object	What is the meaning of the object? Why did you choose it?	Which theme or big idea does it symbolize?
Object 1			
Object 2			
Object 3			
Object 4			

Transformation

Model Lesson: Altered Books

Model Lesson Overview

Students experiment with putting together material in new ways by working with discarded books and transforming the meaning of the words on the page. They choose specific letters, words, or sentences, and they color or paint over the rest of the page, allowing the chosen words to stand out and give new meaning. Students then alter the books, giving new form and meaning by transforming them artistically. They explore how visual art elements such as color, texture, and composition communicate meaning and mood and work with text to communicate an overall message.

Standards

K–2

- Uses descriptive words to convey basic ideas

- Uses a variety of basic art materials to create works of art and express ideas and feelings

3–5

- Uses descriptive and precise language that clarifies and enhances ideas (e.g., concrete words and phrases, common figures of speech, sensory details)

- Knows how different materials, techniques, and processes cause different responses from the viewer

6–8

- Uses descriptive language that clarifies and enhances ideas (e.g., establishes tone and mood, uses figurative language, uses sensory images and comparisons, uses a thesaurus to choose effective wording)

- Knows how the qualities and characteristics of art media, techniques, and processes can be used to enhance communication of experiences and ideas

Materials

- Discarded books

- Art materials (paint, paper, stamps, scissors, glue, ribbon, buttons, etc.)

- *Reflection for Altered Books* (page 232, reflection.pdf)

Transformation (cont.)

Preparation

Familiarize yourself with the many techniques used in altering books by searching for images online that showcase altered books. Bookmark images that can be easily shared with students. Gather discarded books for students to alter. Plan ahead and ask your school and/or local librarians for books that they plan to discard. Decide whether you will take pages out of one book and have students alter one page only or if you would like each student to begin a long-term project of altering an entire book of his or her own over time. Be sure to check discarded books for appropriate content. Additional ideas are provided in the Specific Grade Level Ideas.

Procedure

1. Explain to students that they will have the opportunity to transform, or change, the meaning of a page in a book. Share images of altered books from the Internet, and show students how altered books are showcased in museums.

2. Read aloud any page from a discarded book. Discuss the meaning of the page with students. Model how to give the page new meaning as you choose letters, words, or sentences on the page that combine to make a new thought or create new meaning. Underline or circle the words. They do not need to be in order; you can create meaning with words that are scattered about the page.

3. Discuss the meaning of the words you have chosen. Use art materials such as paint, markers, or colored pencils to cover everything else on the page except the words.

4. Tell students that the page is now a fresh canvas. Using students' suggestions, continue to alter the page with paper, paint, collage, or other media. Tell students that the purpose is to examine how the words and artwork work together to communicate a message to the reader.

5. Provide students with art supplies and a page (or a book) to alter. Discuss how students will repurpose the books that would have been thrown away. Have students sketch plans on a separate sheet of paper to explore a range of possible ideas, noting that artists and writers often experiment with ideas. Use the Planning Questions to help students think about potential directions for their altered books.

6. Monitor students as they work and ask how they are choosing colors and textures to enhance meaning.

Transformation *(cont.)*

7. Distribute *Reflection for Altered Books* (page 232) to students and have them consider how they will transform the meaning of the page or book. Talk about this as a class before asking students to complete the page on their own. Then, have students transform the pages.

8. Debrief the process with students by using the Questions for Discussion.

Planning Questions

- What theme will you explore in your page or book?

- What words or phrases stand out to you?

- How will you alter the meaning of a page?

- What choices will you experiment with in terms of color, shape, cutouts, and additional materials to be collaged into the book?

- How do texture and color speak to you?

Questions for Discussion

- Discuss the dual roles of author and artist you played in the creation of your altered book.

- What choices did you make in both roles?

- How were they similar and different?

- What new meaning did you give to the page or book?

- What artistic techniques produced the most interesting results?

- What is communicated by the composition of the pages?

- What did you learn during the process of creating your altered page or book?

Transformation *(cont.)*

Specific Grade Level Ideas

K–2

Locate discarded books with large print. Have students look for sight words. For example, they can create an altered page all about the word *and*. Students can also create alphabet books, exploring words that begin with specific letters by locating words and images throughout the book that begin with that letter and transform the page accordingly. Explore a particular theme that students can research through image, text, and found materials. Have them select ideas they want to explore further by composing pages in a book. Students could work on single pages that get re-bound in an altered class book.

3–5

Have students share their work in a "silent celebration." Have each student place his or her altered book page on a desk next to a blank sheet of paper for student comments. The blank sheet of paper should have two columns: viewer's name and viewer's comments. Ask students to move from desk to desk, viewing the altered pages and writing comments. Before the celebration, brainstorm ideas for comments as a class such as commenting about how a particular color may make them feel or the artist's choice of words. Remind students that this is a celebration and a time to give positive feedback only, not a time for constructive feedback or criticism. After the celebration, allow time for students to talk with their peers about the work they viewed.

6–8

Students can identify a theme for their altered book and design pages based on this topic. Students can also choose one or more writing pieces from their writing folders and incorporate excerpts into the altered book. As students think about composing a page, they should consider where to place text, what size the text should be, and how images can connect to, expand on, or contrast with the text. Ask students to consider their multiple roles as author, artist, and graphic designer as they construct their books. Explore unifying themes for the book such as mythology.

Name _____ Date _____

Reflection for Altered Books

Directions: Consider the meaning of the pages before and after you transform a book. Record your ideas in the chart.

Before
What was the meaning on the page before you transformed it?

Transformation Process
What artistic choices did you make to transform the meaning?

After
What is the meaning of the page now?

References Cited

Albers, Donald J., Gerald L. Alexanderson, and Constance Reid, eds. 1990. *More Mathematical People: Contemporary Conversations*. New York: Harcourt Brace Jovanovich.

Albers, Peggy, and Jerome C. Harste. 2007. "The Arts, New Literacies, and Modality." *English Education* 40 (1): 6–20.

Andersen, Christopher. 2004. "Learning in 'As-If' Worlds: Cognition in Drama in Education." *Theory into Practice* 43 (4): 281–286.

Association of College & Research Libraries. 2011. "ACRL Visual Literacy Competency Standards for Higher Education." Accessed October 10, 2012. http://www.ala.org/acrl /standards/visualliteracy.

Bellisario, Kerrie, and Lisa Donovan with Monica Prendergast. 2012. "Voices from the Field: Teachers' Views on the Relevance of Arts Integration." Unpublished manuscript. Cambridge, MA: Lesley University.

Bogard, Jennifer M., and Mary C. McMackin. 2012."Combining Traditional and New Literacies In a 21st-Century Writing Workshop." *The Reading Teacher* 65 (5): 313–323.

Brouillette, Liane, and Lynne Jennings. 2010. "Helping Children Cross Cultural Boundaries in the Borderlands: Arts Integration at Freese Elementary Creates Cultural Bridges." *Journal for Learning through the Arts* 6 (1). http://www.escholarship .org/uc/item/1kf6p9th.

Burnaford, Gail, with Sally Brown, James Doherty, and H. James McLaughlin. 2007. *Arts Integration, Frameworks, Research and Practice*. Washington, DC: Arts Education Partnership.

Cahill, Bryon. 2006. "Ready, Set, Write!" *Writing* 29 (1): 12.

Cappiello, Mary Ann, and Erika Thulin Dawes. 2013. *Teaching with Text Sets*. Huntington Beach, CA: Shell Education.

Carpenter, Siri. 2010. "Body of Thought: How Trivial Sensations Can Influence Reasoning, Social Judgment, and Perception." *Scientific American Mind* 38–45.

Center for Applied Special Technology, The. Accessed October 10, 2012. http://www.cast. org/about/index.html.

Collins, Anne M. 2012a. *50 Leveled Math Problems Level 5*. Huntington Beach, CA: Shell Education.

———. 2012b. *50 Leveled Math Problems Level 6*. Huntington Beach, CA: Shell Education.

Collins, Polly. 2008. "Using Poetry throughout the Curriculum." *Kappa Delta Pi Record* 44 (2): 81–84.

References Cited (*cont.*)

Coulter, Cathy, Charles Michael, and Leslie Poynor. 2007. "Storytelling as Pedagogy: An Unexpected Outcome of Narrative Inquiry." *Curriculum Inquiry* 37 (2): 103–122.

Cremin, Teresa, Kathy Goouch, Louise Blakemore, Emma Goff, and Roger Macdonald. 2006. "Connecting Drama and Writing: Seizing the Moment to Write." *Research in Drama Education* 11 (3): 273–291.

Dacey, Linda. 2012a. *50 Leveled Math Problems Level 1*. Huntington Beach, CA: Shell Education.

———. 2012b. *50 Leveled Math Problems Level 2*. Huntington Beach, CA: Shell Education.

———. 2012c. *50 Leveled Math Problems Level 3*. Huntington Beach, CA: Shell Education.

———. 2012d. *50 Leveled Math Problems Level 4*. Huntington Beach, CA: Shell Education.

Dacey, Linda, and Rebeka Eston. 2002. *Show and Tell: Representing and Communicating Mathematical Ideas in K–2 Classrooms*. Sausalito, CA: Math Solutions.

Deasy, Richard J. 2002. *Critical Links: Learning in The Arts and Student Academic and Social Development*. Washington, DC: Arts Education Partnership.

Diaz, Gene, Lisa Donovan, and Louise Pascale. 2006. "Integrated Teaching through the Arts." Presentation given at the UNESCO World Conference on Arts Education in Lisbon, Portugal, March 8.

Donovan, Lisa, and Louise Pascale. 2012. *Integrating the Arts Across the Content Areas*. Huntington Beach, CA: Shell Education.

Dunn, Sonja. 1999. "Just What Is a Chant?" Accessed October 10, 2012. http://www.songsforteaching.com/sonjadunn/whatisachant.htm.

Elliott-Johns, Susan E., David Booth, Jennifer Rowsell, Enrique Puig, and Jane Paterson. 2012. "Using Student Voices to Guide Instruction." *Voices from the Middle* 19 (3): 25–31.

Gardner, Howard. 2011. *Frames of Mind: The Theory of Multiple Intelligences*. 3rd ed. New York: Basic Books.

Griss, Susan. 1994. "Creative Movement: A Language for Learning." *Educational Leadership* 51 (5): 78–80

Hamilton, Martha, and Mitch Weiss. 2005. *Children Tell Stories: Teaching and Using Storytelling in the Classroom*. Katonah, NY: Richard C. Owen Publishers.

Heagle, Amie I., and Ruth Anne Rehfeldt. 2006. "Teaching Perspective-Taking Skills to Typically Developing Children through Derived Relational Responding." *Journal of Early and Intensive Behavior Intervention* 3 (1): 1–34.

References Cited (cont.)

Hetland, Lois. 2009. "Nilaja Sun's 'No Child'...: Revealing Teaching and Learning through Theater." *Teaching Artist Journal* 7 (1): 34–39.

Hetland, Lois, Ellen Winner, Shirely Veenema, and Kimberly Sheridan. 2007. *Studio Thinking: The Real Benefits of Visual Arts Education*. New York: Teachers College Press.

Hourcade, Juan Pablo, Benjamin B. Bederson, and Allison Druin. 2003. "Building KidPad: An Application for Children's Collaborative Storytelling." *Software: Practice & Experience* 34 (9): 895–914.

Hughes, Janette. 2007. "Poetry: A Powerful Medium for Literacy and Technology Development." *What Works? Research into Practice* (October 2007). http://www.edu.gov.on.ca/eng/literacynumeracy/inspire/research/hughes.pdf.

Jensen, Eric P. 2001. *Arts With the Brain in Mind*. Alexandria, VA: Association for Supervision and Curriculum Development.

———. 2008. *Brain-Based Learning: The New Paradigm of Teaching*. 2nd edition. Thousand Oaks, CA: Corwin Press.

Kennedy, Randy. 2006. "Guggenheim Study Suggests Arts Education Benefits Literacy Skills." *The New York Times*, July 27.

Kolb, Gayla R. 1996. "Read with a Beat: Developing Literacy through Music and Song (Teaching Reading)." *The Reading Teacher* 50 (1): 76–77.

Kuta, Katherine. 2003. "And who are you?" *Writing* 25 (5): 30–31.

LaBonty, Jan. 1997. "Poetry in the Classroom: Part I." *The Dragon Lode* 75 (3): 24–26.

LaBonty, Jan, and Kathy Everts Danielson. 2004. "Reading and Writing Poetry in Math." *Reading Horizons* 45 (1): 39–54.

Lane, Barry. 1992. *After THE END: Teaching and Learning Creative Revision*. Portsmouth, NH: Heinemann.

Lyon, George Ella. 2010. "Where I'm From." Accessed March 2, 2010. http://www.georgeellalyon.com/where.html.

Marzano, Robert J. 2007. *The Art and Science of Teaching: A Comprehensive Framework for Effective Instruction*. Alexandria, VA: ASCD.

McKim, Elizabeth, and Judith W. Steinbergh. 1992. *Beyond Words: Writing Poems With Children: A Guide for Parents and Teachers*. Brookline, MA: Talking Stone Press.

National Governors Association Center for Best Practices and Council of Chief State School Officers. 2011. *Common Core State Standards Initiative: The Standards*. Accessed October 10, 2012. http://www.corestandards.org/the-standards.

References Cited *(cont.)*

New, David. 2009. "Listen." National Film Board of Canada video, 6:21. Accessed October 10, 2012. http://www.nfb.ca/film/listen.

Norfolk, Sherry, Jane Stenson, and Diane Williams. 2006. *The Storytelling Classroom*. Westport, CT: Libraries Unlimited.

O'Neill, Cecily. 1995. *Drama Worlds: A Framework for Process Drama*. Portsmouth, NH: Heinemann.

Paquette, Kelli R., and Sue A. Rieg. 2008. "Using Music to Support the Literacy Development of Young English Language Learners." *Early Childhood Education Journal* 36 (3): 227–232.

Partnership for 21st Century Skills. 2011. Accessed October 15, 2012. http://www.p21.org/.

Perret, Peter, and Janet Fox. 2006. *A Well-Tempered Mind: Using Music to Help Children Listen and Learn*. New York: Dana Press.

Poetry Out Loud. 2012. "Tips on Reciting." Accessed January 10, 2013. http://poetryoutloud.org/poems-and-performance/tips-on-reciting.

Powell, Mary Clare. 1997. "The Arts and the Inner Lives of the Teacher." *Phi Delta Kappan* (Fall 1997).

President's Committee on the Arts and the Humanities. 2011. "Reinvesting in Arts Education: Winning America's Future Through Creative Schools." Accessed January 2, 2013. http://www.pcah.gov/sites/default/files/PCAH_Reinvesting_4web_0.pdf.

Reed, Stephen K. 2010. *Cognition: Theories and Application*. 8th ed. Belmont, CA: Wadsworth Cengage Learning.

Reeves, Douglas. 2007. "Academics and the Arts." *Educational Leadership* 64 (5): 80–81.

Rinne, Luke, Emma Gregory, Julia Yarmolinskyay, and Mariale Hardiman. 2011. "Why Arts Integration Improves Long-Term Retention of Content." *Mind, Brain, and Education* 5 (2): 89–96.

Rose, Todd. 2012. "Learner Variability and Universal Design for Learning." Universal Design for Learning Series video, 15:36. http://udlseries.udlcenter.org/presentations/learner_variability.html.

Singer, Marilyn. 2010. "Marilyn Singer: A WBBT Interview." *Writing and Ruminating: One Children's Writer's Journey* (blog). http://kellyrfineman.livejournal.com/638038.html.

Skoning, Stacey N. 2008. "Movement in Dance in the Inclusive Classroom." *TEACHING Exceptional Children Plus* 4 (6).

References Cited (cont.)

Strauch-Nelson, Wendy J. 2011. "Book Learning: The Cognitive Potential of Bookmaking." *Teaching Artist Journal* 9 (1): 5–15.

Theodorakou, Kalliopi, and Yannis Zervas. 2003. "The Effects of the Creative Movement Teaching Method and the Traditional Teaching Method on Elementary School Children's Self-Esteem." *Sport, Education and Society 8* (1): 91–104.

VanDerwater, Amy Ludwig. 2012. "Chickadee." In *Forest Has a Song*. New York: Clarion Books.

Varlas, Laura. 2012. "It's Complicated: Common Core State Standards Focus on Text Complexity." *Education Update* 54 (4). Alexandria, VA: Association for Supervision and Curriculum Development.

Walker, Elaine, Carmine Tabone, and Gustave Weltsek. 2011. "When Achievement Data Meet Drama and Arts Integration." *Language Arts* 88 (5).

Waters, Sandie H., and Andrew S. Gibbons. 2004. "Design Languages, Notation Systems, and Instructional Technology: A Case Study." *Educational Technology Research & Development* 52 (2): 57–68.

Wohlberg, Meagan. 2012. "Don't let the facts spoil a good story': Storyteller Jim Green to release album on Yellowknife's Gold Range." *Slave River Journal* 18.

Yellin, David, Mary Blake Jones, and Beverly A. DeVries. 2007. *Integrating the Language Arts*. Scottsdale, AZ: Holcomb Hathaway Publishers.

Yew, Jude. 2005. "Collaborative Narratives: Collaborative learning in Blogosphere." Master's thesis, University of Michigan. DOI: 2027.42/39368.

Zull, James E. 2002. *The Art of Changing the Brain: Enriching Teaching by Exploring the Biology of Learning*. Sterling, VA: Stylus.

Note-Taking Tool for Observational Assessment

Date: _____

General Notes							
Questions Asked							
Comments Made							
Student Name							

Arts Integration Assessment Rubric
for English Language Arts

Student Name _____ Date _____

Skill	Beginning	Developing	Meeting	Exceeding
Demonstrates understanding of English language arts concepts and skills				
Demonstrates understanding of art concepts and skills				
Communicates thinking clearly				
Demonstrates creative thinking				

Individual Observation Form

Student Name _____ Date _____

Shows understanding (Check all that apply)

_____ Makes representations or notes to understand more fully

_____ Talks with a peer to understand more fully

_____ Asks teacher questions to understand more fully

_____ Helps others to understand

Explains or justifies thinking (Check all that apply)

_____ Communicates thinking clearly

_____ Uses art forms, words, symbols, and writing to summarize thinking
(Underline communication forms that apply)

_____ Uses content vocabulary

Takes it further (Check all that apply)

_____ Makes connections to previous learning

_____ Elaborates on artwork beyond expectations

_____ Suggests new English language arts connections

_____ Creates multiple correct responses to task

Printed with the permission of Shell Education (Collins 2012a, 2012b; Dacey 2012a, 2012b, 2012c, 2012d)

Group Observation Form

Student Name _____ Date _____

Use this form to record scores, comments, or both.

Scores: 1—Beginning   2—Developing   3—Meeting   4—Exceeding

Suggests at least one appropriate task solution				
Works cooperatively				
Supports others in their learning				
Communicates clearly, uses correct vocabulary, and builds on the ideas of others				
Provides leadership/ suggestions to group				
Group Members				

Recommended Resources

ArtsEdSearch
   http://www.artsedsearch.org/

Embodiment: Inferring Theme

Arnosky, Jim. 2008. *Dolphins on the Sand*. New York: G. P. Putnam's Son.

Bahr, Mary. 1992. *The Memory Box*. Morton Grove, IL: Albert Whitman & Company.

Bregoli, Jane. 2008. *The Goat Lady*. Gardiner, ME: Tilbury House Publishers.

Bunting, Eve. 1999. *I Have An Olive Tree*. New York: HarperCollins.

dePaola, Tomie. 1979. *Oliver Button Is a Sissy*. Orlando, FL: Harcourt Brace & Company.

DeRolf, Shane. 1996. *The Crayon Box That Talked*. New York: Random House.

Grover, Jan Zita. 2008. *A Home for Dakota*. Edina, MN: The Gryphon Press.

Hurst, Carol Otis, and Rebecca Otis. 2000. *Friends and Relations: Using Literature with Social Themes Grades 3–5*. Greenfield, MA: Northeast Foundation for Children.

Johnston, Tony. 1988. *Yonder*. New York: Dial Books.

Kraus, Robert. 1971. *Leo the Late Bloomer*. New York: HarperCollins Children's Books.

Library of Congress
   http://www.loc.gov

Lyon, George Ella. 2011. *All the Water in the World*. New York: Atheneum/Richard Jackson Books.

McDonnell, Patrick. 2011. *Me…Jane*. New York: Little Brown & Company.

Polacco, Patricia. 1990. *Thunder Cake*. New York: Putnam & Grosset Group.

Smith, Lane. 2011. *Grandpa Green*. New York: Roaring Book Press.

Stead, Philip C. 2012. *A Home for Bird*. New York: Roaring Book Press.

Steig, William. 1971. *Amos and Boris*. New York: Farrar, Straus and Giroux.

Waber, Bernard. 1975. *Ira Sleeps Over*. San Anselmo, CA: Sandpiper.

Yezerski, Thomas F. 2011. *Meadowlands: A Wetlands Survival Story*. New York: Farrar, Straus and Giroux.

Recommended Resources (cont.)

Interpretation: Inferring a Character's Feelings

Baylor, Byrd. 1986. *I'm in Charge of Celebrations*. New York: Aladdin Paperbacks.

Bunting, Eve. 1988. *How Many Days to America? A Thanksgiving Story*. New York: Clarion Books.

Mills, Lauren. 1991. *The Rag Coat*. New York: Little Brown Books for Young Readers.

Moving Statues: Strong Verbs

Macken, Joann Early. 2008. *Flip, Float, Fly: Seeds on the Move*. New York: Holiday House.

Rosen, Michael. 2010. *Tiny Little Fly*. Somerville, MA: Candlewick Press.

Spinelli, Eileen. 2000. *Song for the Whooping Crane*. Grand Rapids, MI: Eerdmans Books for Young Readers.

Choreography: Life Cycle Books

Bang, Molly, and Penny Chisholm. 2009. *Living Sunlight: How Plants Bring the Earth to Life*. New York: The Blue Sky Press.

DePalma, Mary Newell. 2005. *A Grand Old Tree*. New York: Arthur A. Levine Books.

Frost, Helen. 2008. *Monarch and Milkweed*. New York: Atheneum Books for Young Readers.

Kalman, Bobbie. 2007. *The Life Cycle of an Emperor Penguin*. The Life Cycle Series. New York: Crabtree Publishing.

Sayre, April Pulley. 2008. *Trout Are Made of Trees*. Watertown, MA: Charlesbridge.

Teacher-in-Role: Photographer's Snapshots with Words

Bregoli, Jane. 2008. *The Goat Lady*. Gardiner, ME: Tilbury House Publishers.

Bunting, Eve. 1994. *Night Tree*. New York: Voyager Books.

George, Jean Craighead. 2011. *The Buffalo Are Back*. Pine Plains, NY: Live Oak Media.

Library of Congress
http://www.loc.gov

MacLachlan, Patricia. 1987. *Sarah, Plain and Tall*. New York: Harper Trophy.

Recommended Resources *(cont.)*

Velasquez, Eric. 2010. *Grandma's Gift*. New York: Bloomsbury Publishing.

Yolen, Jane. 1987. *Owl Moon*. New York: Philomel Books.

Tableaux: Vocabulary Words

George, Jean Craighead. 2008. *The Wolves Are Back*. New York: Dutton Children's Books.

Thompson, Lauren. 2008. *Hope Is An Open Heart*. New York: Scholastic Press.

Waber, Bernard. 2002. *Courage*. New York: Houghton Mifflin Company.

Enacting Scenes: Using Reading Strategies

Stein, David Ezra. 2010. *Interrupting Chicken*. Somerville, MA: Candlewick Press.

Monologue: Meet the Character

Roddy, Ruth Mae. 2000. *Minute Monologues for Kids*. Rancho Mirage, CA: Dramaline Publishing.

Stevens, Chambers. 2009. *Magnificent Monologues for Kids 2: More Kids' Monologues for Every Occasion*. South Pasadena, CA: Sandcastle Publishing.

Georgia O'Keeffe Texts

Bryant, Jen. 2005. *Georgia's Bones*. Grand Rapids, MI: Eerdmans Books for Young Readers.

Lasky, Kathryn. 2009. *Georgia Rises: A Day in the Life of Georgia O'Keeffe*. New York: Melanie Kroupa Books.

Novesky, Amy. 2012. *Georgia In Hawaii: When Georgia O'Keeffe Painted What She Pleased*. New York: Harcourt Children's Books.

O'Keeffe, Georgia, and Britta Benke. 2006. *Georgia O'Keeffe: The Artist in the Desert*. New York: Prestel Publishing.

Rodríguez, Rachel. 2006. *Through Georgia's Eyes*. New York: Henry Holt and Company.

Venezia, Mike. 1993. *Getting to Know the World's Greatest Artists: Georgia O'Keeffe*. Danbury, CT: Children's Press.

Winter, Jeanette. 1998. *My Name Is Georgia: A Portrait by Jeanette Winter*. New York: Voyager Books.

Recommended Resources (*cont.*)

Improvisation: Characters Come to Life

Rueda, Chris. 2006. *Let's Play in the Forest*. New York: Scholastic Press.

Wordless Texts

Bang, Molly. 1980. *The Grey Lady and the Strawberry Snatcher*. New York: Simon & Schuster.

Day, Alexandra. 1985. *Good Dog, Carl*. New York: Simon & Schuster.

Lee, Suzy. 2008. *Wave*. San Francisco, CA: Chronicle Books.

Lehman, Barbara. 2004. *The Red Book*. New York: Houghton Mifflin Books for Children.

———. 2007. *Rainstorm*. New York: Houghton Mifflin Books for Children.

———. 2011. *The Secret Box*. New York: Houghton Mifflin Books for Children.

Newgarden, Mark, and Megan Montague Cash. 2007. *Bow-Wow Bugs a Bug*. New York: Harcourt.

Pinkney, Jerry. 2009. *The Lion and the Mouse*. New York: Little, Brown and Company.

Raschka, Chris. 2012. *A Ball for Daisy*. Schwartz and Wade Books.

Found Sounds

Galbraith, Kathryn. 2011. *Planting the Wild Garden*. Atlanta, GA: Peachtree Publishers.

Rocco, John. 2011. *Blackout*. New York: Hyperion Books.

Songwriting: Understanding a Tall-Tale Character

Naylor, Phyllis Reynolds. 2011. *Emily's Fortune*. New York: Yearling.

Chants: Main Idea in Nonfiction Narratives

George, Jean Craighead. 2008. *The Wolves Are Back*. New York: Dutton Children's Books.

———. 2011. *The Buffalo Are Back*. Pine Plains, NY: Live Oak Media.

Sayre, April Pulley. 2011. *Rah, Rah, Radishes! A Vegetable Chant*. San Diego: Beach Lane Books.

Recommended Resources (cont.)

Mash-Up: Meaningful Memories

Velasquez, Eric. 2004. *Grandma's Records*. New York: Walker Publishing Company.

Soundscapes: Exploring Settings

Aardema, Verna. 1992. *Bringing the Rain to Kapiti Plain*. New York: Puffin Books.

Ward, Helen. 2003. *The Tin Forest*. New York: Dutton Children's Books.

Dialogue Poems: Compare and Contrast

Bidner, Jenni. 2006. *Is My Dog a Wolf? How Your Dog Compares to Its Wild Cousin*. Asheville, NC: Lark Books.

Fleischman, Paul. 2004. "Fireflies." In *Joyful Noise: Poems for Two Voices*. New York: Harper Trophy.

The Poem Farm
http://www.poemfarm.amylv.com

Rhyme and Rhythm: Writing and Performing Poetry

Dunning, Stephen, Edward Lueders, and Hugh Smith, comps. 1967. *Reflections on a Gift of Watermelon Pickle*. New York: Willam Morrow & Company.

Frost, Robert. 1916. "The Road Not Taken." In *The Poetry of Robert Frost*. New York: Henry Holt and Company.

Juxtaposition: Word Bowls and Found Poems

National Geographic Kids™. Tampa, FL: National Wildlife Geographic Society.

Ranger Rick. Reston, VA: National Wildlife Federation.

TIME® for Kids. New York: TIME for Kids.

Reversos: Two Sides to Every Story

Singer, Marilyn. 2010. *Mirror Mirror: A Book of Reversible Verse*. New York: Dutton Juvenile.

Recommended Resources (cont.)

Personification: Nonfiction Literature

Bang, Molly, and Penny Chisholm. 2009. *Living Sunlight: How Plants Bring the Earth to Life.* New York: The Blue Sky Press.

———. 2012. *Ocean Sunlight: How Tiny Plants Feed the Seas.* New York: The Blue Sky Press.

Exaggeration: Two Truths and One Exaggeration

Jenkins, Steve. 1998. *Hottest, Coldest, Highest, Deepest.* New York: Houghton Mifflin.

The Untold Story: Historical Fiction

Denenberg, Barry. 1997. *So Far From Home: The Diary of Mary Driscoll, an Irish Mill Girl.* New York: Scholastic.

Gregory, Kristiana. 2006. *Across the Wide and Lonesome Prairie: The Diary of Hattie Campbell, The Oregon Trail, 1847.* New York: Scholastic.

Larson, Kirby. 2010. *The Fences Between Us: The Diary of Piper Davis, Seattle, Washington, 1941.* New York: Scholastic.

McKissack, Patricia C. 2003. *A Picture of Freedom: The Diary of Clotee, a Slave Girl, Belmont Plantation, Virginia, 1859.* New York: Scholastic.

Pinkney, Andrea Davis. 2011. *With the Might of Angels: The Diary of Dawnie Rae Johnson, Hadley, Virginia, 1954.* New York: Scholastic.

Collaborative Storytelling: The Twisting and Turning Plot

Creech, Sharon. 2002. *The Wanderer.* New York: HarperCollins.

O'Malley, Kevin. 2005. *Once Upon a Cool Motorcycle Dude.* New York: Walker Publishing Company.

Visual Patterns: Signature Characteristics

American Library Association
http://www.ala.org

Cain, Janan. 2000. *The Way I Feel.* Seattle, WA: Parenting Press.

Marcus, Leonard S., ed. 2012. *Show Me a Story! Why Picture Books Matter: Conversations with 21 of the World's Most Celebrated Illustrators.* Somerville, MA: Candlewick Press.

Recommended Resources *(cont.)*

Representation: Graphic Novels

Alley, Zoe B. 2010. *There's a Princess in the Palace*. New York: Roaring Brook Press.

Mixed Media: Life Stories Told and Retold

Juster, Norton. 2005. *The Hello Goodbye Window*. New York: Hyperion Books.

Smith, Lane. 2011. *Grandpa Green*. New York: Roaring Brook Press.

Contents of the Digital Resource CD

Page Number	Resource Title	Filename
N/A	Correlation to the Standards	standards.pdf
30	Embodiment Brainstorming Guide	embodimentguide.pdf embodimentguide.doc
31	Observing Others	observingothers.pdf observingothers.doc
36	Movement Ideas	movementideas.pdf movementideas.doc
37	Character's Feelings	feelings.pdf feelings.doc
42	Movement Words and Phrases	wordsandphrases.pdf
48–49	Choreography Planner	choreographyplanner.pdf choreographyplanner.doc
50	Pathways	pathways.pdf
56–57	Six Qualities of Movement Reference Sheet	qualitiesmovement.pdf
58	Movement Phrase Graphic Organizer	movementgo.pdf
69–70	Sample Scenario	samplescenario.pdf
71	Snapshots in Stories	snapshots.pdf
77	Gallery Walk Observation Sheet	gallerywalk.pdf gallerywalk.doc
81	Drama Planner	dramaplanner.pdf dramaplanner.doc
86	Georgia O'Keeffe Monologue Sample 1	monosample1.pdf
87	Georgia O'Keeffe Monologue Sample 2	monosample2.pdf
88	My Notes	mynotes.pdf mynotes.doc
89	Monologue Planner	monoplanner.pdf monoplanner.doc
94	Getting Ready for Improvisation	improvisation.pdf improvisation.doc
104	Our Sound Words	soundwords.pdf soundwords.doc

Contents of the Digital Resource CD (cont.)

Page Number	Resource Title	Filename
108–109	The Ballad of Johnny Appleseed	ballad.pdf
N/A	"The Ballad of Johnny Appleseed"	balladjohnnyappleseed.mp3
N/A	"The Ballad of Johnny Appleseed" Instrumental Version	instrumentalappleseed.mp3
110	Lyric Brainstorming Guide	lyricguide.pdf lyricguide.doc
111	Songwriting Planner	songwriting.pdf songwriting.doc
116	Sample Chants	chants.pdf
117	Planning for Chant	planningchant.pdf planningchant.doc
122–123	Interview Planner	interviewplan.pdf interviewplan.doc
128	The Sounds of a Setting	sounds.pdf sounds.doc
138–139	Examples of Dialogue Poems	exampledialogue.pdf
140	Two Voices Poem Plan	twovoices.pdf twovoices.doc
144	Tips for Performing Poetry	tipspoetry.pdf
145	Marking the Meaning	meaning.pdf meaning.doc
149	Found Poem Example	foundexample.pdf
154	I Am From Example 1	iamfromexample1.pdf
155	I Am From Example 2	iamfromexample2.pdf
156	I Am From Planner	iamfromplanner.pdf iamfromplanner.doc
160	Reverso Sample	reverso.pdf
161	Reverse These Lines	reversetheselines.pdf reversetheselines.doc
172	Character Development Planner	characterplanner.pdf characterplanner.doc

Contents of the Digital Resource CD (cont.)

Page Number	Resource Title	Filename
176	Fact Collector	factcollector.pdf factcollector.doc
177	Scenario Planner	scenarioplanner.pdf scenarioplanner.doc
178	Sample Storytelling Techniques	storytellingtech.pdf
184	Diary Entry	diaryentry.pdf diaryentry.doc
185–186	Diary Samples	diarysamples.pdf
191	Retelling Plan	retellingplan.pdf retellingplan.doc
196	The Plot Twister	plot.pdf plot.doc
206	Digital Story Planning Guide	digitalstory.pdf digitialstory.doc
207	Storyboard Planner	storyboard.pdf storyboard.doc
211–212	Finding Patterns	patterns.pdf patterns.doc
218	Graphic Novel Hunt	novelhunt.pdf novelhunt.doc
219–221	Graphic Novel Templates	noveltemplate.pdf noveltemplate.doc
226	Creating Interview Questions	questions.pdf questions.doc
227	Mixed Media Catalog	mixedmedia.pdf mixedmedia.doc
232	Reflection for Altered Books	reflection.pdf reflection.doc
238	Note-Taking Tool for Observational Assessment	notetaking.pdf
239	Arts Integration Assessment Rubric for English Language Arts	assessmentrubric.pdf

Contents of the Digital Resource CD (cont.)

Page Number	Resource Title	Filename
240	Individual Observation Form	individualform.pdf
241	Group Observation Form	groupform.pdf

Acknowledgments

We are extremely grateful for the dedication and hardwork of the many individuals who have shaped this book. As such, we would like to give special thanks to the following individuals:

David Williams for your amazing songwriting, singing, and poetry

Mary C. McMackin, Ed.D.

MSAD 35 Superintendent Dr. Mary Nash

MSAD 35 Teachers

Jerry Burnell, Principal

Ann Marie Townsend, Children's Librarian, South Berwick, ME

Humble ISD Teachers and Assistant Superintendent Cathy Airola

Rob Bogard

Rick Donovan

Mary Ann Fraser for teaching through the arts

—Lisa and Jennifer

Notes

Notes

Notes